CALLED TO CARE

Encounters with Faith in the Field of Nursing

Bonnie Hunt MSN, RN

InspiringVoices®

Inspiring Voices books may be ordered through
booksellers or by contacting:

Inspiring Voices
1663 Liberty Drive
Bloomington, IN 47403
www.inspiringvoices.com
1 (866) 697-5313

Because of the dynamic nature of the Internet, any web addresses or
links contained in this book may have changed since publication and may
no longer be valid. The views expressed in this work are solely those
of the author and do not necessarily reflect the views of the publisher,
and the publisher hereby disclaims any responsibility for them.

Any people depicted in stock imagery provided by Thinkstock are
models, and such images are being used for illustrative purposes only.
Certain stock imagery © Thinkstock.

ISBN: 978-1-4624-1035-4 (sc)
ISBN: 978-1-4624-1036-1 (hc)

Printed in the United States of America.

Inspiring Voices rev. date: 09/04/2014

Contents

Just a
Nurse

Just a Nurse?

The chemotherapy room was quiet, except for an occasional beep from an infusion pump. Two patients were dozing in recliners. The third, Mrs. Watkins, was fidgeting in her purse for a paperback to read. Mr. Watkins was sitting quietly beside his wife watching the *drip, drip, drip* of his wife's first chemotherapy treatment intently. The morning had been busy for nurse Ruth Owens. She had been assessing her patients, checking their port-a-caths and had started their chemotherapy. She finally sat down to do the necessary paper work, but her eyes continually swept the room to check on her patients.

Suddenly, a look of terror crossed Mrs. Watkins' face. She clasped her chest and uttered, "I can't breathe."

Her eyes rolled back as her head slipped to the side. Realizing her patient was having an anaphylactic reaction, Ruth leapt from her chair, pressed the emergency button, discontinued the chemotherapy, slipped an oxygen mask on Mrs. Watkins and wrapped a blood pressure cuff around her arm. Almost immediately, another nurse came into the room and Ruth ordered her to administer an antihistamine to stop the allergic reaction and cortisone to decrease the inflammation that was blocking the airway. Before the emergency team arrived, Mrs. Watkins' breathing returned to normal and the look of terror had faded.

Ruth turned to the three ashen-faced onlookers and said quietly, "It's frightening to see something like this. But it is under control."

Still shaken, but with color returning to his face, Mr. Watkins returned to the chair beside his wife and looked at Ruth inquiringly, "Are you a doctor?"

"Oh no! I'm just a nurse," replied Ruth.

"We need a nurse in room 202," a nursing assistant called to the nurses' station.

Nurse Jim Hayes hurried down the hall to room 202 to find Mrs. Green diaphoretic and saturated in perspiration from head to foot. Quickly assessing the situation, he asked her if she was diabetic. With a nod "yes" from Mrs. Green, Jim immediately obtained a finger stick blood sugar of 47. A call to the lab was placed. The tech said they were busy with an emergency but would come as soon as possible. After Mrs. Green drank orange juice with added sugar, the finger stick blood sugar was repeated: 51.

Several rounds of orange juice and an hour later, Mrs. Green's blood sugar was 79. Gown and bed linens already changed, the lab tech finally arrived, drew blood and called back verifying the blood sugar was now 79. Checking to find the cause of Mrs. Green's drop in blood sugar, Jim discovered that she had had her 5:30 p.m. NPH insulin but was not hungry so did not eat her supper.

"Any time you take your NPH insulin, you must eat your recommended diet and have a bed time snack," Jim reminded Mrs. Green.

As Jim left the room, the patient thanked Jim stating she felt a lot better and then admonishes, "Young man, why don't you go to medical school and become a doctor?"

Members of Southern Scholars had gathered for a seminar class to discuss

Virginia Wolfe's book, *A Room of One's Own*, which was spurned by the inequality of opportunities for female writers due to lack of financial independence and a place to be creative. She made a compelling argument about the lack of encouragement and recognition women received for their talents and accomplishments, particularly in the literary world. Even though the book was written in the early part of the twentieth century, it was chosen to center the discussion on issues women face in today's society. I was asked to moderate the discussion. While we were waiting for the seminar to begin, I overheard the students' conversations about what they would be doing after graduation.

A senior nursing student responded to the question of what she planned to do with her degree, "Well, I am not going to be 'just a nurse.'"

In the light of the topic for this particular discussion and astonished at her reply, I blurted out, "There is no such thing as 'just a nurse.'"

There are millions of nurses making a significant impact on health care. A recent American Nurses Association slogan, "Every patient needs a nurse" reflects the need for nurses in society. When asked whom they trust most out of all the health care professionals, the public rated nurses highest. A survey on who the public perceives as the most honest of all professions, not just in health care, nurses were still rated number one.

And let us not forget that Jesus' ministry was not only to preach the gospel but also to bring comfort and healing to the brokenhearted and the suffering. Since it is "nursing" care that brings about healing, I'd like to think of Jesus as a community health nurse, for He went about Galilee

"...preaching in the open air and healing people of every kind of sickness." Matthew 4: 23.

Also, the apostle Paul reminds us, "There are different ways of serving the Lord, but all the gifts are given to honor Him... It's true that there are different [spiritual] gifts...[some] are given a special measure of faith; another is given the gift of *healing*; and so on--all are given by the Holy Spirit." 1 Corinthians 12:5,9

Each of us is not "just a nurse"! It is a special spiritual gift.

Just a Nurse: Same Song Second Verse

A friend of mine who is dedicated, competent and has her master's in nursing, said her husband had been complaining, "You might know a lot about nursing but not much else."

The embarrassment from realizing how true that might be brought to mind all the times a bunch of us nurses got together and all we talked about was nursing.

Defensively, I boasted to myself, *So, if we know only a lot about nursing and not much else, just look at all we do.* I have long been an advocate for promoting nursing by emphasizing the vital role of nurses in health care. Nurses catch errors before they can happen; nurses can take pulmonary artery pressures with one hand while comforting the patient with the other; nurses deliver babies; nurses hang out their shingle and have their own practices; nurses save lives. I could go on, but you get the picture. Because of all the good we do, the complaint of my friend's husband not only stirred up embarrassment but a bit of resentment. Intuitively, I knew then we are much more than "just a nurse."

Then, I read a devotional book for women by women and often would read the author's biographical sketch. Over time, it struck me how many nurses had contributed to this book and how multidimensional they were. I felt vindicated.

Well! I thought to myself, *just look at all that these nurses know besides nursing.*

The short biographies of the nurses that contributed to just one years' devotional book reflected accomplishments far beyond the field of nursing. Their hobbies included the usual: gardening, travel, music, handwork, exercise, and reading. Then, there were scuba divers, oil painters, writers, kayakers, wake boarders, and rock climbers, too! Feeding backyard lake inhabitants like fish, duck, birds, and worms, however, amused me the most—quite a show of dedication to the environment.

Several of the registered nurses had earned Master's degrees in fields outside of nursing such as religion, business, counseling and education. Many held leadership positions in various organizations. Some were directors of women's ministries and other church offices. One even served on the executive committee for a Christian business and professional women's club. Another contributor was a case manager for the seriously mentally ill, volunteered for the "Make-a-Wish" foundation, produced a monthly newsletter, handled public relations for a church and Kiwanis club. Some homeschooled their children, while another taught driver's education, and, of course, many assisted husbands in their careers.

The writers captured my attention. The majority of the biographies revealed that there were serious writers among us. Not just the nurses that had contributed to the devotional book, but others who had been published in a variety of ways. They contributed to church papers, newspapers, and magazines. One even had a recent book of miracle stories, answered prayers, and angel encounters published in addition to contributing to the aforementioned publications. There was even a woman who was associate editor of a Christian woman's magazine and a poetess.

Even though my sampling of nurses was very, very, small, I still wanted to say, *See, we are a lot more then 'just a nurse'* and take seriously Ecclesiastes 9:10 which says, "Whatever you do, give it everything you've got and enjoy it."

Life is Backwards

Beep, beep, beep.

It was Mrs. Mackey's TPN running low this time. It seemed that every time I passed Mrs. Mackey's room a piece of her equipment would call for my attention. Earlier, it was her PCA pump that needed a refill. Then, it was one of her infusion pumps that beckoned for a new bag of IV fluids. After that, it was time to switch piggybacks from IV antibiotics to Pepcid. Then, Reglan. Then, she needed another antibiotic. Each time I entered her room, Mrs. Mackey would stir a little and, through the haze of her illness, peer at me. I would inquire as to how she was feeling and if there was anything else I could do for her. Her reply varied from, "I am not bouncing back from this surgery like I should," to, "I just feel too bad to know if I even need anything else."

Since Mrs. Mackey had been too ill and too weak to be ambulatory, her physician had ordered that this afternoon, she must get out of bed and walk in the room. With a few *ooohs* and *ouch* moans, she stood at the side of the bed and walked a few paces around the room. As I put her back to bed, I tried to arrange the pillows and her position to make her as comfortable as possible. Washing my hands after emptying her bulging Foley catheter bag, I was off to check on my other patients and try to meet their needs before the end of my shift.

Beep, beep, beep.

Oh no! Now one of Mrs. Mackey's infusion pumps was yelling, *Occlusion! Occlusion!* I quietly entered the room and found she was lying on the tubing, compressing the flow. As gently as I could, I coaxed the tubing free and started to clear the infusion pumps for the end of the shift when Mrs. Mackey stirred again and peered at me.

"Life is all backwards," she whispered.

"How's that?" I responded.

"Look at the wages of football players and entertainers compared to nurses and teachers." Weakly, she continued, "Just think of the contribution that nurses and teachers make to society."

Then, she turned back to her comfortable side and seemed to drift off to sleep.

As I completed my chores for the end of the shift, the phrase "life is all backwards" kept running through my mind. I thought to myself, *Yes, life is all backwards in many aspects of life and nurses certainly are not exempt from this backwardness.*

An editorial in the *St. Paul Pioneer Press* by Laura Billings aptly pointed out this backwardness. It was entitled, *Wanted:*

Good pay for quite a few good nurses. It seemed that the Minnesota Nurses Association was asking to raise the base pay for full-time nurses to something more reasonable then their present status. Surprisingly, the public seemed to think the wage increase was not merited and decided to voice their opinion with comments like, "Nurses don't even know how good they've got it."

You can say that only if you know nothing about nursing, the editorial pointed out. It then went on to say, "Let's review the job description: 'Wanted: a compassionate and highly skilled caregiver willing to work evenings, weekends and major holidays, solving stressful problems (i.e. life or death) in highly collaborative environment, risking repeated exposure to everything from hepatitis to HIV, and working with a patient population sicker than ever before. Heavy lifting, constant hand-holding and occasional housekeeping (blood, urine, etc.) required.'"

I think we could all agree that society does have some backward tendencies. I don't often think about the inequities of nurses' pay scale (not to say we shouldn't give it more thought). However, after reading Laura Billings' job description of a nurse, I felt validated for having chosen such a lofty profession. In reflecting on our lofty profession and the "backward value" issue, a thought came to me, *Do we as nurses have our values backward? Do the demands of our career cause us to neglect the "first things first" value?*

"...make God's kingdom and His righteousness first in your life..." Matthew 6:33. "You should love the Lord your God with all your heart, all your soul and all your mind." Matthew 22:37.

Some years ago, I remember reading a compelling thought in a daily devotional book: men do not order God out of their lives. That is, not many do. Our lives are just so cluttered up with day to day living that we have no time for Him. In our spare time we might serve God and attend worship when nothing else interferes. The things we are doing may be all right and good, yet, here the good becomes an enemy of the Best.

Putting "first things first" is not the result of chance. Sometimes, we have to ask God to provide the time for us to prioritize. This commitment brings its own reward. The Bible tells us not to worry about what to eat or what to drink or what to wear in Matthew 6:31, because if we make God and His kingdom first, all those things will be given to us as we need them.

Making God first is the secret to reversing the "life is all backwards" syndrome.

Thank a Nurse

Over the years, I collected stories about nurses that inspired me and used them as a worship thought before class would begin for my students. One such story was from an article by Linda Chitwood.

Ms. Chitwood tells about Josh being born with a severely damaged brain. The only cry that came from the delivery room was the weeping of his mother. Josh was admitted to an intensive care unit.

"His crib was shadowed by the best medicine could offer, yet nothing could medicine off this child. Revolutionary treatment, sophisticated monitors, talented doctors—they could do nothing for this child."

So, when it became time for the mother and child to go home, A NURSE orchestrated the bonding between the baby and his mother; a NURSE taught Mary to feed Josh through his stomach, since he could neither suck nor swallow; a NURSE taught Mary suctioning and seizure management; a NURSE tramped through the mud to an isolated clapboard shack to demonstrate formula preparation in a home without electricity or running water; a NURSE comforted Mary when Josh died; a NURSE arranged for the pauper's burial.

Ms. Chitwood chided, "and you thought nurses just carried out doctors' orders."

She continues with, "Thank a NURSE for noticing that the doctor has been ordering IV potassium supplements but hasn't checked a serum level in days. Thank a NURSE for averting a near disaster when different doctors ordered conflicting treatments.

Thank a NURSE for comforting a patient with one hand while measuring pulmonary artery pressures with the other. Thank a NURSE for calming anxious relatives when no one wanted to fool with them. Thank a NURSE for monitoring the patients all night while you slept soundly. Thank a NURSE for explaining what the doctor didn't have time to."

Ms. Chitwood concluded her article by urging us not to "forget it was a NURSE who made a difference in Josh's life; not a neurosurgeon, not a CAT scanner, a NURSE. NURSES give their love and their lives. Let's give them the respect they deserve."

Thank you, Ms. Chitwood, for being our advocate.

Dr. Thomas, physician and author of the book *The Youngest Science,* writes of his high respect of nursing as a profession. An illness that required an extended hospital stay clued him into things about nurses that his physician friends did not know:

"The institution is held together, glued together, enable to function as an 'organism' by nurses and by nobody else. They spot errors before errors can be launched. It takes a confident, competent and cheerful nurse, in and out of the room on one chore or another through the day and night, to bolster one's confidence that the situation is indeed manageable and not about to get out of hand."

He closes his chapter on nurses with "knowing what I know, I am all for the nurses. If they want their professional status enhanced and their pay increased, if they ask for the moon, I am on their side.

Thank you, Dr. Thomas, for also being on our side.

GOD is on our side too. He encourages us to "not become tired of doing good, for in time, we'll reap the spiritual harvest if we don't give up." Galatians 5:9

Never
Give Up

Failure That Works

His quiet, unassuming manner, large teddy bear-like build and shy smile endeared Jesus (pronounced "Hay-Suse") not just to me but to all the faculty. To say he was a favorite would be quiet accurate.

Jesus wanted to be nurse; it was his goal, and he went about his nursing education with great determination. But, life is seldom without its difficulties and Jesus was not exempt. Jesus was working full time to pay his tuition and help support his parents, who had immigrated, financially. His family responsibilities of accompanying his parents, who spoke very little English, to doctor appointments, car repair appointments, and often needing to arbitrate when job difficulties arose, was taking a toll on his education.

One day, he entered my office dressed neatly and fashionably and with his shy smile said, "I need your help."

Thus began a friendship and journey neither of us could have ever anticipated. Regular study sessions were scheduled. Even with his tight schedule, Jesus was always prompt with his appointments, and his aspiration for nursing and appetite for learning never wavered. Jesus seemed to have a good grasp of the concepts of nursing, but testing was his nemesis. It was not without many "ups and downs" and sundry setbacks (failing and repeating a course) that Jesus' nursing education was finally behind us. (I say "us" because in my business of "assisted learning" it feels like an "us" effort. I take it rather personally if a struggling, but faithful, student does not do well.)

If there was word to describe Jesus' graduation, it would be "jubilation." Family, faculty, classmates and friends joined in the celebration with hugs and well wishes.

The next hurdle was passing the NCLEX (National Council Licensure Examination) in order to practice as a registered nurse. He followed the prescription for preparing for this exam, meeting with me on a regular basis, reviewing nursing content and practicing questions. With great trepidation, anxiety and prayer, Jesus sat for the exam. The results? Not so good. To cheer him up I said, "Let's look on the bright side, you can take the exam again in ninety days (now it every 45 days) and we will review more and more NCLEX practice questions."

This we did. The results: bad news again.

"Well, Jesus we are going to keep at this and in ninety days you can take the exam again."

I learned that phrase well by repeating it every ninety days over the next three years.

I also went through the grieving process with Jesus. After each failure Jesus would say, "I feel like the end of the world has come."

Then, he would shut the door to his room and not talk to anybody for a few days, pleading with God to give him wisdom and guidance on what to do. He asked God, "Do You want me to be nurse?"

Even though he felt the end of the world had come for him, Jesus remarked that something deep down in his soul continued to encourage him that nursing was still the direction God wanted him to go.

After four or so failures, Jesus, who had continued working at a bakery job, decided that even if he had to work as an orderly, the hospital work might help him. Into the picture comes a guardian angel in the form of a nurse manager, Sue. Sue immediately saw Jesus' potential. He was neat, professional, had good critical thinking skills and was eager to learn. After a few weeks of orderly work, Sue had Jesus working as a nurse tech, and then elevated him to work as a graduate nurse under the supervision of an RN preceptor in anticipation of his passing the NCLEX exam he was to take in ninety days.

With the ninety days up and some excellent hospital experience behind him, with continued practice sessions with me and at home on his computer, with much encouragement and many prayers from coworkers and family, Jesus went to take the exam in his most optimistic mood. Results: depressing. The good news was Sue, the nurse manager, still had faith in Jesus' potential and continued to let him work under the supervision of an RN. He was respected and well liked by the nursing staff as well as by physicians, patients and their families.

Let's fast forward to more failures (seven altogether) and three years after graduation.

The time limit was up. There was just one more chance in this particular state. By now, Jesus was reviewing and practicing questions on his own with just an occasional session from me.

After taking the national exam for the eighth time and three years after graduating with his AS degree in nursing, I found Jesus in an optimistic mood saying he had taken all 265 questions. Now, he was looking up his results on the computer every day. There were a few anxious days not only for Jesus but for the family, faculty, friends and nurses at the hospital who had petitioned God on Jesus's behalf over those trying years. Finally I received a call from Jesus.

"We did it," was all he could get out at the moment.

I asked him what his first thoughts were when he saw his "active" status on the computer screen.

Humorously he replied, "Now I don't have to sit in front of that computer and answer practice questions anymore!"

Coming by to show me the print out of his "active status" from the computer, he commented, "I feel I am the most blessed nurse around! I have had so much support from faculty, family, fellow nurses and, of course, God. I can see how all the studying and reviewing has given me an edge many other nurses do not have. For with each failure I had to study and review more and now I have a great base of knowledge that has made me very comfortable with my practice of nursing. I have no regrets, just thankfulness that the Lord had been with me through those trying years."

Jesus' promise to his disciples in Matthew 28:20, "I'll always be with you, even until the end of the world," is very real to Jesus (Hay-Suse). Is it real to you? It can be if you trust His word.

All those years of prepping for the national nurses exam paid off. In the hospital where Jesus worked, he was known as the "smart" nurse. The smart nurse title could have been reward enough, but not for Jesus.

With his Associate's degree in nursing and the national exam behind him, Jesus marched right back to school graduating with his Bachelor's of Science in Nursing in a year and a half. Without missing a beat, it was onward to a Master's degree. Now, as a respected, bilingual Family Nurse Practitioner working in a family practice clinic, Jesus' opportunities are limitless.

What kept Jesus' courage from eroding into total despair during those difficult years?

"I know the plans I have for you. Plans to prosper and not harm you: to give you a future and a hope." Jeremiah 29:11 was the promise that lifted him above the mire of failure.

The Virtue of Observation

It was one of their first nursing clinicals and still unsure of themselves, Lynn and Jan were delighted to be assigned the same patient. That way, they felt, they could pool their limited knowledge and resources. The patient, Mr. Howe, was an easily confused gentleman in his late seventies. After introducing themselves, Lynn took his temperature, counted his pulse and respirations and Jan took his blood pressure. Next, they took turns following their assessment instructions. Using their penlights, they checked Mr.

Howe's pupils; using their stethoscope they checked breath sounds, abdominal sounds and felt for pedal pulses. With the assessment completed, the girls chatted with Mr. Howe, asking about his health history and about his family while they waited for the breakfast tray to arrive. When it came, Lynette spread Mr. Howe's toast with jam while Jan opened his juice and silverware, placing the napkin on his lap. Drinking his orange juice and consuming the scrambled eggs and toast with gusto, the girls noted that Mr. Howe did not suffer from a poor appetite.

After he finished breakfast, the girls had planned to give him his bed bath but decided to provide mouth care first. They looked in the bedside table for a toothbrush, toothpaste and emesis basin. There was none. They looked over the bedside table. None. They searched on top of and in each drawer of a chest of drawers that was in the room. Nothing. The bathroom didn't have any of the items either. Finally they asked Mr. Howe if he knew where his toothbrush was, but he didn't.

Jan went to the supply room and retrieved a new set of mouth care supplies. They set up a glass of water and emesis basin, put toothpaste on the toothbrush and handed it to Mr. Howe. Instead of taking the toothbrush with paste as expected, he startled them by saying, "How can I brush my teeth when you forgot to put them in this morning?"

Even though Lynette and Jan's classmates had a big chuckle over the incident, they lamented, "What kind of nurses are we going to be if we can't even notice a patient doesn't have teeth?"

It took a few days, but the girls began to see the incident as a catalyst for improving their assessment skills and were encouraged by looking at Galatians 6:9 in a very practical way: "Let's not become tired of doing good for in time, we'll reap [better assessment skills] if we don't give up."

Disillusioned

"You need to write a devotional on disillusionment," sighed Brandi, a recent nursing graduate who was in orientation at a children's emergency department. She knew I was writing devotional stories for nurses.

"No one told me it would be like this. I had no idea I would feel so inadequate. And to think I thought God wanted me to be a nurse!"

"What do you want me to write?" I inquired.

"Let me tell you what happened to me in just one shift, the one I worked yesterday: First I went to the PIXES (a medicine and equipment dispensing machine) and pulled out a SPLINT and brought it to the room where my preceptor was waiting for the SLING she had requested. Keeping everyone waiting, I had to run back, return the splint and, again, key into the PIXES for a SLING and bring it back to my harried preceptor.

Next, we were trying to start an IV on a very fragile child and missed. I got a new IV needle for my preceptor to try again. She successfully "hit" the vein and asked me to hand her the "T" connector and tubing. *Oh no!* I screamed in my head. I had put the used needle with 'T' connector in the sharps box and thrown the tubing in the trash. There was my preceptor putting pressure on the vein so it wouldn't bleed out the needle and I was running to the PIXES again to get the new equipment. Unfortunately, there was someone replacing the supplies in the PIXES who did not feel the same urgency that I felt and made me wait until she was finished.

Next, I was to give directions for a child to go to nuclear medicine; mistakenly, I gave the parents the directions to X-ray. Later, I had to transport a child with her mother in tow to nuclear medicine. I was reading the signs to make sure I was going in the right direction and pushed the gurney right into a cart in the hallway, jarring the child. I know that mother wondered if I knew what I was doing." Brandi continued,

"Do you think Satan is trying to discourage me? On top of all this, the nurses are so critical of each other and the other health care providers. My mother warned me that 'nurses eat their young.' I feel all eaten up."

It was no smiling matter to Brandi, but I couldn't help but smile thinking that every nurse alive could probably relate to a similar tale of horror.

As faculty, we encourage dedication as well as competency and teach to a high standard. The result? Graduates who enter the working world with a great deal of idealism and a desire to be competent, compassionate nurses. Professional nursing has tremendous challenges that can discourage the rookie nurse as in Brandi's case.

It is inspiring to have a fresh and creative look at nursing through philosophy papers that first-year nursing students write. Surprisingly insightful concepts already resonate with these novices such as "The Health Care Industry would be worthless without one component: THE NURSE!" Other students made the point that nursing is not a piece of paper, or a few letters after your name, or a white uniform; it is a mindset, a commitment to care for others. The most basic of abilities bestowed on us, is a responsibility that represents symbols of God's love: a devoted pair of hands for

His work to be ministered through. Since I was inspired by these comments, I shared them with Brandi.

We talked about how, hopefully, the good days will outweigh the bad days and to always keep in mind that

"With God, anything is possible." Matthew 19:26.

Also, Paul encourages us in Galatians 5:9

"Let's not become tired of doing good, for in time, we'll reap the spiritual harvest if we don't give up."

Brandi ended our conversation with, "All I really want to do is be a really good nurse!"

Florence

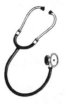

She was born with a "silver spoon in her mouth," so the saying goes. Her wealthy parents, the Nightingales, had homes in London and in the English countryside. Ambitions for their daughters were "the good life": social events, travel, needlework, music, and drawing.

Parthenope, one of their daughters, took to the good life like a duck to water, but this was not so for Florence—she was a very unhappy camper. She wanted to be a nurse.

This unconventional ambition horrified her parents. Why, only the poor took their sick to the hospital and "privileged" young ladies would never work in institutions that were so loathsome and unsanitary.

Undaunted by the conventional wisdom of the day, Florence tried to persuade her parents to let her work in a nearby hospital. With her parents' adamant refusal of the idea, Florence settled into a miserable, depressed state, longing for a life of service in relieving the "sufferings of man" and caring for those with disease. It was during this time that Florence rejected a marriage proposal stating she had a "passionate nature, which required satisfaction. This nature could not be satisfied by spending a life with him in making society and arranging domestic things." Her refusal to marry further infuriated her parents. To boost her sagging spirits, Florence covertly read books about nursing and hospitals. She came upon information about a reputable hospital in Kaiserswerth, Germany that was run by deaconesses that were skilled in nursing. Elated, she secretly cherished thoughts that one day she would be able to train as a nurse there.

It was a stroke of luck, or more likely providence that family friends invited Florence to vacation with them in Europe. They were aware of her secret interest in the Kaiserswerth hospital and indicated they would arrange a visit to Kaiserswerth if she accompanied them on this trip. After her visit to Kaiserswerth and observing the routines and techniques by the doctors and nurses for several weeks, Florence returned home feeling so brave, as if nothing could ever vex her again. However, vexation returned. Her parents were furious when they found out she had visited Kaiserswerth. Now, they insisted that she be a companion to her sister, going for rides in the country, drawing, singing, and doing needlework. "I have no desire now but to die," wrote Florence in her journal.

About a year after her visit to Kaiserswerth and after many a stormy argument, Florence was grudgingly allowed to return to Kaiserswerth and train as a nurse. The rest is history.

After studying at Kaiserswerth, Florence returned to London with the highest of recommendations, for it was said that no one had so thoroughly mastered the art of nursing and had passed the exam with so great of distinction as Miss Nightingale. She became superintendent of a London hospital that catered to the genteel.

Then, it was off to the Crimea War, where she is credited for saving the lives of thousands of sick and wounded soldiers by improving the sanitary conditions in military field hospitals. Not only was Florence's brilliant administrative abilities demonstrated during her service in the Crimea war, but so was her compassionate nature. Late into the night after her administrative and nursing duties were completed, Florence would light her lamp and make her way to the bedside of wounded soldiers, providing comfort and words of encouragement. Thus, she became known as the "lady with the lamp."

After returning to London as a national heroine, Florence spent her time promoting hospital administration and reform. She later founded the Nightingale School and Home for Nurses.

I wrote this short tribute of Miss Florence Nightingale lest we forget to credit her for elevating the quality of nursing education and the status of nurses in England and here in America that still resonates today.

I once read that Florence felt she was called of God to a life of service. Undaunted by obstacles that could have been insurmountable and her parents' adamant objections, Florence pursued that call. With the bad press nursing gets—overworked, underpaid, not appreciated—I wonder how many, today, would have the same tenacity to persevere in becoming a nurse if they encountered the same setbacks as Florence.

"And we know that God causes everything to work together for the good of those who love him and are called by Him." (Romans 8:28)

American Dream

It was a rush job for me with one of my students. As Academic Assistance Coordinator for nursing majors, I was to assist Letica with a small contract she needed to finish before graduation weekend started that evening. The gloomy afternoon, and the fact Letica had this contract to finish before she could leave for home after graduation could have put a wrinkle in anyone's disposition, but not Letica.

"Are your parents here already?" I asked.

"They were leaving my home in Missouri just as I was coming over to your office. Even though it is a 14-hour drive, they are so excited because this is the first graduation they have ever attended. In fact, this is first graduation in our family period."

Attractive, stylish, ambitious, motivated and ardent student are all words I would use to describe Letica, so the story of Letica's family that she so humbly told me came as a surprise.

Her parents were mere teenagers— her dad had a 7th grade education and mom a 9th grade education— when they emigrated from Mexico to Missouri. Hot sun, tedious work and calloused hands were souvenirs her Dad acquired working as a "laborer" with a landscaping company. Her mother earned her income by cleaning other people's houses. The long hours and tiresome labor did not diminish her dad's desire to succeed and provide for his wife and, eventually, his two daughters.

Surprisingly, in a few years, he was able to establish his own small landscaping company that flourished under God's guiding hand and her dad's faithfulness in tithing. With great appreciation and humility, Letica explained that the neighborhood where her family resided was not the most desirable, but their home was the most "beautiful" in that area and was debt-free. They also had a second beautiful home, also debt-free, in Mexico. This was used for family gatherings during holidays.

Because of her parents' frugality and faithfulness in depending on God's wisdom in their lives, they were able to provide Letica and her sister a very comfortable lifestyle. Vacations, besides going to their home in Mexico, included traveling around Europe, Australia, the Bahamas, Hawaii, Canada, the United States and most recently, the Holy Land of Israel. When it was time for Letica to go to college, she chose the university of her choice without concern about tuition cost. She also came equipped with the latest technology, which contributed to achieving her goal of nursing.

After telling her story, she added that her mother did not have to, but still did, clean houses so she could feel like she was making a contribution to the family. Letica wanted to clarify that not only did her parents provide well for her and her sister, but her parents' generous spirit had helped many non-family members financially.

After graduating with her Associate of Science in nursing, Letica continued on and received a Baccalaureate degree in nursing. Now with her Master's degree, Letica's confident, competent, and caring nursing skills as an oncology nurse certainly is making a significant impact on the role of a nurse.

The reason I wanted to tell Letica's story is because this American dream has provided a productive, competent member for the nursing profession, and that legacy will live on for years to come.

I feel that Letica's dad found strength in Philippians 4:13, which says, "I can face any situation with Christ who gives me strength" and Philippians 4:19, "My God will supply all your needs from His glorious riches which, because of Jesus Christ, now belong to you."

Kindness— It's a Good Thing

Too Busy to Help?

In addition to being knee-deep into a family nurse practitioner program, Laura and Bodil were working full-time and had family responsibilities. Frequently, they rode to class together, chatting about their work, their families or the class. And often, they would pray together asking God to help them to not be so consumed with their plight that they neglect to help someone in need.

Driving to class one afternoon, Laura and Bodil were somewhat preoccupied discussing the upcoming pharmacology class and soon-to-be responsibility of prescribing drugs. The truck in front of them was slowing them down and they did not want to be late for class. Even though it was just a two-lane road, Laura looked for a single yellow line in hopes of passing the truck. Then, she noticed that the driver of the truck was slumped to the right of the steering wheel and then leaned way over to the left of the wheel. He kept swaying back and forth as he drove ahead of them.

"Bodil! Look at that man in the truck, I think something is wrong with him!" Laura shouted.

About that time the truck started to cross the yellow median line into oncoming traffic.

Laura blared her car horn in hopes of alerting the driver of the truck of the danger and warning on coming traffic. The truck slowly drifted back in his lane, but now the driver was slumped down onto the seat. Again the truck started to move erratically from lane to lane. Laura stayed very close behind the truck continuing to blow her horn. The driver lifted his head every so often but did not stop his scary behavior. A tunnel was just around the bend and Laura knew that the man's driving was a tragedy waiting to happen if something wasn't done soon. Silently praying for guidance, Laura crossed the median line ever so slightly, frantically blowing her horn and flashing her lights to warn the oncoming traffic, while still trying to get the driver's attention.

Miraculously, the truck drifted to the right shoulder just before entering the tunnel and came to a halt in a ditch.

Laura pulled to the shoulder behind the driver. Bodil ran to call for help as Laura rushed up to the driver's side of the truck. She opened the door and asked the man what was wrong. He muttered,

"I'm diabetic," and then slumped motionless on the seat of the truck.

Laura remembered that there were some Oreo cookies in her car. She ran back to her car and grabbed a hand full of cookies. Splitting the cookies in half, she wiped the white filling onto her finger and then rubbed it around the gums of this motionless man.

Soon the police arrived and called for the paramedics. After transferring the man to the rescue vehicle, the paramedics started an IV and rushed him to the hospital. Satisfied the man was in good hands, Laura and Bodil continued on to class.

Unfortunately, the busyness of our lives so often preoccupies us with our own needs that we neglect reaching out to others. Like Laura and Bodil, we need to pray that we are not so self-absorbed that we do not respond to someone in need.

"When you who have possessions and see a brother or sister in need but you don't help him, how can you say that you love God?" 1 John 3:17

First Clinical Jitters

"Can you be excited and scared to death at the same time?" asked Melita. "The answer is 'yes.' It happened to me," she exclaimed as she told me the story of her very first hospital clinical in nursing school.

"I set my alarm in time to get up early so I would have time to shower, dress with everything tucked in and in its proper place and eat a good breakfast in preparation for my first hospital clinical experience. As I settled in for a good night's sleep, I checked the alarm again and, yes, it was properly set. When I snuggled so 'comfy' under the covers, I began to yawn, hoping to drift into a much needed sleep. Instead of sweet sleep, I tossed and turned, throwing the covers off because I was too warm and yanking them back up because I was chilled. About every hour, I checked the time to make sure the alarm was still set. I felt as if 'fear' was vying for the 'excitement' of tomorrow's events. I was so excited about going to the hospital to put into practice what I had learned, but still worried silly. Would I really be able to bathe and change the bed linens while the patient assigned to me remained in bed? Would I administer the right medicines at the right time? Would my patient like me? I guess this was a classic case of first clinical jitters.

When the alarm finally went off at 5:00 a.m. I literally jumped out of bed. Feeling less than rested, I attempted to eat breakfast. I chewed my Cheerios just enough so that I could swallow them without choking. Now it was time for me to don the uniform I had been so eager to wear. *Oh no!* I muttered to myself as my heart sank. There, hanging in the closet, as it should have been, was my new, but wrinkly, uniform. In my excitement of the evening before, I forgot to iron my uniform. Ironing my uniform would not have been a problem, except that I could not find my iron. After a frantic search of my room, it dawned on me a friend had borrowed it. I really did not want to disturb my friend at this early morning hour, but necessity prevailed.

With my uniform pressed, I took one last glance at myself in the mirror. I actually felt like a nurse now and wondered why I even bothered going to clinicals that day. Then, fear crept in again, and the same worries from the night before came flooding back.

Well! When I finally got to the hospital, the RN assigned to my patient reported to me that my patient was elderly, didn't have any legs, was deaf, and didn't talk.

This report did nothing to soothe my fears. However, I did manage to bathe her and change the bed linens without incident. But giving her medications was a different story. I don't know whether she just didn't like me or maybe it was the pills, but she spit them out and they flew to the floor. Now I wondered what to do. Pick them up and administer them again? *No*, I reasoned, *I wouldn't want that done to me.* I tried to remember if something like this had been discussed in class. Nothing came to mind. I went to the nurses' station and found my nurse and asked her what I should do. She instructed,

'Just pick them up and try giving them to her.'

I wasn't sure I had heard her correctly, so I got my courage up and asked her what to do again. Same response: "Just pick them up and give them to her."

Even though my poor patient had dementia and wouldn't know the difference,

I decided I'd better look for my instructor. Thankfully, she informed me there was a very simple solution to my problem. She helped me pour out some new pills that we administered. This time, my patient swallowed them without difficulty."

Melita concluded her story by informing me her first clinical day in the hospital taught her that sadly, not every nurse goes by what our books say. Then she added, "Good thing I was that patient's nurse that day!"

Like Melita, most of us encounter first time jitters. Peaceful nights of sleep evade us as fear nudges images of our human frailties into our conscience. But we have something great going for us: God has given us many, many promises to hold onto in situations where we need assurance and strength, in times of crisis and in ordinary everyday events. One in particular is found in Isaiah 41:13-14 where God promises, "I am the Lord your God. I will strengthen you and hold your hand, so do not be afraid... Don't fear my children, I will help you."

About those pills on the floor, not putting aside the sanitary issue, Melita did come up with a basic principle all of us should put into practice: don't do it if you wouldn't want it done to you (Matthew 7:12). Then at the end of the day, maybe, just maybe, the patient will appreciatively say,

"Good thing you were my nurse today!"

Gifts Differing

"We really made a striking couple. Bill with his lopsided grin and me hobbling around from my hysterectomy," mused Helen as she was telling me about her husband's parotid surgery and her recent hysterectomy.

Helen had barely been discharged from the hospital when her husband had to go in for his surgery. Since I have a burden concerning the image of nursing, I asked Helen what had impressed her most from these two recent hospital experiences.

Grinning from ear to ear, she recounted an incident that occurred early one morning as she was returning to Bill's room from the cafeteria with her breakfast tray.

"This man from housekeeping saw me hobbling down the ground floor hall with my hands full."

"I see you need some help," he observed.

"Then, he held the elevator door. I entered, thinking that was nice of him to hold the door for me but his kindness did not end there. He also entered the elevator, pushed the button to my floor and went up the four flights with me, and then held the door open for me to exit and wished me a good day. I was expecting this gentleman from housekeeping to get off on this floor with me for a chore he had to do. But no, he helped me off and went back down to the ground floor to finish his chores there."

Helen insists that people are frightened when they come to the hospital and are acutely aware of how each hospital personnel, from the person in admissions to the person that cleans the room to the person that discharges them, treats them.

"There were a few snafus, but the care was good and most everyone was pleasant, but the memory of the kindness of the man from housekeeping is what has stayed with me," said Helen as she concluded her comments.

I didn't get the image of nursing I hoped for, but I did get the picture of what a user-friendly institution should be.

Paul tells us in Romans 12:7-11 that we have been given "gifts differing."

"If you have received the gift of pastoral concern, then do that. Or, if you have the gift of teaching, then concentrate on that. If God has given you the gift to counsel and encourage others, do it. If you have the gift of administration, take your responsibilities seriously. If you've been given the capacity to show kindness and compassion, do it joyfully." Paul adds, "Be kind and courteous to one another as true brothers and sisters, honoring each other above yourselves. Don't be lazy; do your work enthusiastically, just as if the Lord Himself had employed you."

Jesus Cares

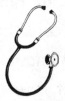

Hunger, thirst and headache competed in the war against much needed sleep. Not only was sleep elusive but the patient's courage was shrinking. Chest pain has a way of putting a damper on even routine surgery and that is how Mrs. Hager found herself on the cardiac unit. With the surgery canceled, Mrs. Hager remained NPO (nothing per oral) for more then 48-hours in anticipation of rescheduling her surgery.

But first, various test had to be completed in hopes of discovering the source of her chest pain. A nurse had given Mrs. Hagar a couple of Tylenol with a sip of tepid water for her headache.

"I finally fell asleep, but every time I turned over in bed, I was reminded how badly my head still hurt," lamented Mrs. Hager.

"Mrs. Hager, Mrs. Hager do you need more Tylenol?"

Mrs. Hager said she tried to open her eyes but the over head light caused her to squint and all she could see was the name on the nurse's badge: Jesus.

"Don't you have any water to take with these pills?"

Explaining that she had not had anything to eat or drink for a couple of days the nurse responded, "Let me go check on something."

He came back with a small cup of ICE water with a straw, "You need a little water."

"I took a sip of the water to swallow the Tylenol and I believe it was the best stuff I had ever had," reported Mrs. Hager.

As the nurse stood there, she looked at his badge again and commented, "I know you probably pronounce your name 'Hay-Suse' but as far as I am concerned, right now you are JESUS and this is LIVING WATER."

He patted her arm and said he hoped she felt better soon, turned off the light and left the room.

"Wow!" thought Mrs. Hager, *God has placed me on a unit where a man named Jesus brought me a much needed cup of water to assure me without a doubt that He still loved me and that He was still in control.*

"Lord, Jesus," she prayed, "I love you and I pray that I never, ever forget or fail to mention the ways that You have loved me. Thank you for taking care of me. Thank you for caring. Thank you for a cup of ice water."

**Jesus (Hay-Suse) is the same nurse in the story "Failure That Works."

Good Medicine

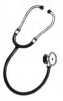

"Laughter is the sun that drives winter from the human face," Victor Hugo.

Some might surmise there is little to laugh about when providing nursing care for the sick and suffering. Wrong! Sometimes, it is those very incidents that make us smile that keep us from buckling under the stress.

It seems a travesty to me now, but in the olden days, parents were only allowed to visit their hospitalized child on Tuesday and Thursday afternoons for an hour. So, five-year-old Johnny was left alone in his hospital crib the evening prior to his surgery for strabismus. A charming little rascal he was and not the least bit shy. "Chatter box" doesn't do him justice but will have to suffice for the lack of a better phrase. Unfortunately, it was one of those shifts that one hopes is not repeated very often. Running to and fro past Johnny's room would entice him to call out, "Nurse! Nurse! Come in here and play with me."

"I need you nurse," he would then call out after getting no response for a playmate. When one of us would go into his room to see what he wanted he would point to a toy he had thrown out of his bed or say he wanted a sip of water or, "Um, I think I need some medicine."

By the end of the shift, he was still awake but had settled down a bit. Making my last rounds for the evening, I was able to take a few minutes to confront this little charmer and wondered how he was going to react when he came back from surgery the next day with both eyes bandaged.

As soon as I arrived for my shift the next day, I found Johnny sitting somewhat subdued in his crib tugging at the bandages covering both his eyes.

"Oh! Johnny don't touch your bandages, you will undo all the work the doctor has done."

Turning in the direction of my voice he replied,

"Nurse I won't touch these bandages if you will only turn on the lights and pull up the shades."

I don't think I wiped the smile from that statement off my face for days.

There are too many shifts that leave nurses humorless and burnt out, so it is these unexpected humorous moments that buoy us up, even if we have to laugh at ourselves. Like the time a patient rang his call light and the nurse answered,

"May I help you?"

"Can you come down here?" the patient asked.

"I'll be there in a minute," she said.
"Is that a real minute or a nurse's minute?"

Mary, a nursing assistant, went to check on a patient that was due to go for a test and was NPO (nothing per oral). The patient's granddaughter, who was in her 30's was sitting at her bedside. The granddaughter asked if it was OK to wipe her grandmother's head with a damp washcloth.

That's fine, Mary responded.

The granddaughter replied, "I know I can't put it by her mouth."

Confused, Mary asked her why. Her answer, "The sign on the door says 'Nothing by Mouth.'"

Mary told us she chuckled the rest of the shift.

"Working as a certified nurse assistant in a long term health care facility is not easy, but it is rewarding work," confided Kelly now a nursing student.

However there were incidences that made my work enjoyable. I still get a chuckle over the time I walked into a female resident's room to get her up for the afternoon. As I was getting ready to get her up, I realized I didn't have an adult brief, which she needed. I explained, 'I'll be right back, I need to get a diaper.' As I was leaving the room she called out, 'Honey, bring me one too.'"

Those that work with pediatric patients probably could fill a book with laughter. An ER nurse tells about a precocious four-year-old that was brought to the ER with a chief complaint of cough and difficulty breathing. She kept up a nonstop conversation while the nurse was trying to assess her heart rate and lung sounds. Finally the nurse said,

"Shhh, I have to see if Barney is in there."

The child looked up and calmly stated, "I have Jesus in my heart. Barney is on my underwear."

Then there was Mark, born with one ventricle. He spent much of his childhood in and out of hospitals. This time he was in with fluid overload. He was sneaking so many drinks that they had to lock his bathroom door. He protested but finally settled down to play. He decided to be artistic and set up his paper and paints. It seemed innocent until he asked the nurse to fill this cup with water.

"Very, very cold water, please."

One of my favorite chuckling events occurred while Art Linkletter was touring a nursing home. He approached a sweet white-haired lady in a wheel chair, shook her hand and asked,

"Do you know who I am?"

"No," she replies, "But if you go to the nurses' station they'll tell you who you are."

Humor is a basic human need. Make the humor in your work a health issue. It's a Biblical principle.

"A merry heart is good medicine, but a broken spirit dries out the bones." Proverbs 17:22

Having Done It for One of the Least

Cindi relates:

Understaffed, underpaid, underappreciated!
Understaffed, underpaid, underappreciated!
Understaffed, under paid, underappreciated!

The phrase was bouncing off my consciousness like a rubber ball bouncing up and down on the pavement. I was trying to cope with 30 severely mentally ill adult patients. These clients were incontinent, drooling and hallucinating. Some had dried food on their clothes, some were in fetal position, others were just milling around, and still others were quietly coloring with crayons in coloring books. I had medications to administer and blood glucose sticks with sliding scale insulin to draw up and administer. Then, I needed to chart.

But these people needed some physical care, and more importantly, they needed "tender loving care." I was an agency nurse with one assistant, and to say the task was overwhelming would be an understatement. Then, on top of all this, the assistant added a less than comforting thought— recently one of the patients had stabbed a nurse in the neck.

I complained to the supervisor that I did not have enough help, that the task was just too overwhelming, and I could not see how I was going to cope. Empathetically, she gave me a bit of advice I will never forget.

She said, "Cindi, think of it this way: inasmuch as you have done it unto one of the least of these, you have done it unto Me."

The strangest thing happened: as "inasmuch as you have done it unto one of the least of these, you have done it unto Me" kept resonating in my thoughts, my tension slowly evaporated. I began to think that maybe I would be able to cope with the overwhelming situation.

Even so, my responsibilities were not without its difficulty. Administering medications was very time consuming. I had to patiently coax some patients to open their clamped-shut mouths as I attempted to give them their medicines; others, I had to make sure did not lose some of their medication in their drool; still others shied away from me when they realized a needle stick was eminent. But surprisingly, as the end of the shift approached, the assistant and I had time to get clean clothes on the patients that were incontinent, while making the others comfortable in chairs or couch to watch TV instead of milling around aimlessly. I even sat down and colored a picture with those that had been coloring quietly.

Now as I continue to do agency nursing in a mental health setting, the verses Matthew 25:35-40 anchor me for the challenge: "You have cared about others, which shows that you care about me. When others were thirsty, you gave them water. When they were hungry, you gave them food, and when they were without a place to live, you took them in. When they were sick, you visited and comforted them, and when they were in jail, you didn't forget them... What you did by caring for those who are thought to be unimportant was acknowledged by God as if you had done it for me."

Spiritual Life—First Things First

Living Water

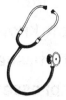

A ramshackle shack of a house on the side of a mountain was the home of an elderly husband and wife, Henry and Della. It didn't seem to matter to them that the house was poorly insulated against the harsh elements and that they did not have indoor plumbing; it didn't seem to matter that the foam rubber in the couch's cushions had crumbling under faded threadbare upholstery; it didn't seem to matter that their kitchen table and chairs wobbled on the uneven wood planks that served as a floor; it didn't seem to matter that the wooden crates used as a kitchen cupboard were as bare as Old Mother

Hubbard's cupboard. They had each other and "dog."

Henry did the best he could to care for Della after she fell and broke her hip. But Henry did not know that continuous pressure on soft tissues between bony prominences compresses capillaries and occludes blood flow causes damage to the underlying tissue. So, the inevitable happened: a pressure ulcer developed on the sacrum. Because of the ulcer, it became necessary for a community health nurse to make daily trips through the mud to the little shack. Kathy was assigned this task. It was during the first visit that a special bond developed between the nurse and this frail elderly couple. Kathy looked forward to her daily visits to provide ulcer care. However, after a few weeks, it became evident that Della's care was too much for Henry. So, arrangements were made for Della to be placed in a long-term health care facility.

Concerned about having to separate this devoted couple, Kathy made a visit to the healthcare facility expecting to find a sad and homesick Della. Instead, sparkling eyes and a grin from ear to ear greeted Kathy as she entered Della's room.

"How are you doing?" asked Kathy.

"Guess what?" Della enthused, "I get corn bread that has butter on it every day and they put me in this big tub where water comes right out of the wall and you can get water anytime you want by turning a knob."

"Della's enthusiasm made her sound as if she was describing the Hilton," Kathy joked.

It was difficult to believe in this age of high technology that one would not be aware that water "comes right out of the wall" and is very accessible just by "turning a knob." I wonder how many of us are like Della—not aware that "living" water is plentiful and always available any time we need it just by turning the knob of prayer?

"Living water" is special. "Once you drink it you will never be thirsty again. It will constantly bubble up inside of you like a fresh mountain spring, furnishing eternal life." (John 4: 14)

If we drink this living water, then we might be just like Della, eyes sparkling and grinning from ear to ear. And shouldn't we share with others, just like Della did with Kathy, that "living water" is plentiful and always available just by turning the knob of prayer?

Postscript:

On another visit, Della shared with Kathy her worries,

"Henry is not doing so good and he refuses to go see a doctor."

It was a sheriff that noticed he had not seen Henry for a few days and went out to check on him. Henry was dead and lying on the floor. "Dog" was lying on top of him growling and showing his teeth daring anyone to come near his master. Della spent her remaining days sad but content, where water came out of the wall and she could get water anytime she wanted just by turning a knob.

Dismayed

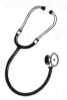

"You cannot imagine the shock it is for patients and family to hear the doctor say, 'You have cancer,'" commented Helen, an oncology nurse.

"I am sure they must feel like the television commercial that says when you hear you have cancer it is like being dropped off a boat, left alone and you don't know how to swim. It is a particular blow when the patient has had no health problems and something shows up during a routine physical. This was the case with Mr. Haynes,"

Helen continued, "It was in a routine laboratory test that an elevated protein was noted which ultimately led to a diagnosis of multiple myeloma. Shock is probably an understatement for what Mr. Haynes and his wife felt when the doctor told them Mr. Haynes' diagnosis. He had just retired and had been in good health with plans for travel and building a winter home in Florida."

Helen carefully and patiently explained what Mr. Haynes was to expect from his first chemotherapy treatment. The first round of chemotherapy was a six months long oral dose followed up with laboratory tests. The Haynes' postponed their plans to go to Florida for the winter and faithfully carried out the prescribed treatment. After six months, laboratory tests revealed protein levels within normal range, so it was off to Florida and a good time for the Haynes. Returning back home for more follow up laboratory tests, the news was disappointing. The protein levels had elevated again.

Now, we are going to have a more aggressive chemotherapy treatment. This round of chemotherapy will be with intravenous drugs. These drugs will cause you to be ill with nausea, vomiting and dizziness and your hair will fall out," warned Helen.

As Helen continued with her instructions, she silently wondered how many patients over the years she had given these very same instructions to and how very ill her patients had become with these particular drugs.

"Even though I knew this precious couple had a strong faith and a faithful prayer life, I felt a particular sadness for what these drugs were going to put them though," related Helen.

During the treatment, Helen called to check on Mr. Haynes. When Helen asked to speak to him, Mrs. Haynes said he was out painting the house. Astonished Helen inquired,

"Is he nauseated?

"No-oo," was the reply.

"Well if he is dizzy, he should not be on a ladder," continued Helen.

"Well he is not dizzy. He is not sick and the house needs painting," responded Mrs. Haynes.

Helen said her disbelief was so compelling, she made several more calls inquiring about Mr. Haynes' condition. Same response: no nausea, no vomiting, no dizziness and no hair falling out.

"I was beginning to feel like I was having a 'Jonah experience' and that the Haynes' would view me as a false prophet because my warnings did not materialize," lamented Helen. "The side effects never did materialize, and it left me completely dismayed."

After tests revealed Mr. Haynes' protein levels had decreased, the Haynes's referred to the experience as "positive faith."

"Prayer and a positive attitude can go a long way," insisted Mrs. Haynes. "The Lord will go with you. He will not forsake you."

As for Helen, Isaiah 55:8-9, "The Lord says, 'My thoughts are not your thoughts, neither are my ways your ways. The heavens are higher than the earth, so are my thoughts higher than your thoughts and my ways higher than your ways,'" took on a new meaning.

Unusual? Maybe Not

They were mingling in the lobby of the nursing building. Their smiles and casual chatter masked the anxiety of the upcoming exam. It had been a tough semester, and this exam was critical for several of their classmates. Graduation was just weeks away.

A few minutes before 9:00 a.m. when the exam was to begin, the students started to file into the student lounge and invited me to join them. They gathered around in a close circle while Jen opened her Bible and claimed several promises.

"For I know the plans I have for you, plans to prosper you and not to harm you, to give you hope and a future. (Jeremiah 29:11)

"Don't be afraid for I am with you... I will uphold you with my victorious right hand." (Isaiah 41:10)

Before bowing their heads to pray, Jen requested, "we need to especially pray for Janice and Barbara since passing this test is so critical for them."

Then we all bowed our heads, and Jen offered a prayer reminding God of His promises and asked for a special portion of wisdom to be given to the two students that were in jeopardy.

"Well, I certainly am touched and impressed!" I commented as we left the lounge.

"Oh! We have done this before every test since we began nursing with EVERY classmate participating," enthused Shannon.

I was curious as to how the class was going to respond when I found out that the two students that they made a special petition for had failed the exam. They seemed a little more anxious but optimistic the next day as they gathered for the final exam. As these students had done all throughout their nursing education, they gathered in the lounge for claiming promises and prayer, and again, made a special request for the two classmates.

Later that day, I saw the students with glorious smiles and thumps up letting me know *all* had passed. With much encouragement and study support from their classmates, the two students that were struggling had made a high enough score on the final to give them a passing grade. These students' faith never wavered for they felt their devotion to claiming promises and prayer would pay off—and it did!

I mused cynically to myself that this class was unusual because it was smaller than most nursing classes, but I was comforted that at least some young people were still seeking God's guidance for their lives.

The notion that this graduating class was unusual was pleasantly shattered the next day as I passed the student lounge and heard the sweet melody of "Nearer, Still Nearer."

"Nearer still nearer, close to Thy heart. Draw me, my Savior, so precious Thou art; fold me, O fold me close to Thy breast, Shelter me safe in that haven of rest," they sang, the melody wafting through the air.

This class of nursing students was preparing for an upcoming exam in the lounge. Their custom was to pick out a favorite hymn, sing, pray, and then give each other encouraging hugs as part of their preparation for each exam.

Yeah! For our future nurses.

"For where two or three gather in my name, there I am in the middle of them." Matthew 18:20

Promises

It had been an intense study session. Since she failed the last test, the upcoming test would be a determining link to Eva's progression in the nursing fundamentals class. A career in nursing had been a lifelong dream for Eva, and the thought of "failing out" was more than she could bear. Turning to me with pleading eyes, Eva explained, "I get so nervous when I take these tests," and then asked, "What do you do about 'test anxiety'?

I try to read all of the assignments and study the notes, but when I get to the test I begin to feel so anxious that when

I look at the choice of answers they ALL look right."

We had already gone over some test-taking techniques like covering up the options, making sure to know what the question was asking, trying to answer the question first and analyzing the options one at a time. We also had talked about the importance of prayer. But at that time, I sensed she needed more encouragement.

I have a folder, which contains some printed sheets of paper on decorative paper that is titled "God's Wonderful Promises to Claim for NCLEX." I pulled one of these sheets from the folder and gave it to Eva, explaining that these were some promises that we give to encourage the students preparing for the National Council Licensure Exam (NCLEX). As she glanced over the promises, she looked at me with the most engaging smile and exclaimed, "We need these now! Don't wait until NCLEX time to give them to us."

I suggested she look them over and memorize one that would be helpful to her. I also told her about a student who wrote her memorized promise at the top of the sheet of paper she used to cover up her answers while she was reading the questions. When she felt anxiety creeping in, she would stop and read the promise, and that calmed her down.

A few days later, Eva was in my office with another student, Melinda, who was agonizing over her test anxiety. I produced another "promise sheet." We sat around for a few minutes looking over the promises with Melinda, trying to decide which promise would comfort her most. Finally, Eva broke the silence, "That very first promise on the sheet gives me tremendous encouragement and is my favorite."

'For I know the plans I have for you. Plans to prosper and not harm you... to give you a future and a hope (Jeremiah 29:11).'"

Then, Eva told Melinda how she wrote that promise down as soon as she started her last test. When she felt anxious, she would stop for a moment and read it. Eva continued, "Even though I always pray for wisdom before each test, claiming this promise during the test kept me focused on God being with me all through the test."

Flashing that irresistible smile of hers, Eva continued, "I passed the test and plan to keep this practice with all my tests. Now, I have confidence that God is giving me a 'future and a hope.'"

"Give all your worries and cares to God, for He cares about what happens to you." 1 Peter 5:7

Claiming His wonderful promises is a great way to give your anxieties, fears and worries to God. Try one today!

Missed Impression

Instructions

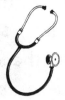

I was making rounds checking on my nursing students and their preceptors when I heard, "Mrs. Hunt! Mrs. Hunt! You won't believe what just happened!"

Oh no, I moaned in my head, *What happened?*

"One of my patients, Mrs. Thomson, is going for surgery tomorrow morning and an order was left for her to scrub her abdomen three times with antiseptic soap. My preceptor handed me a styrofoam cup to fill with antiseptic soap from the floor stock. I filled the cup took it to the Mrs. Thomson's room. She was preoccupied with unpacking and visiting with her family, so

I briefly explained that after her family left, she was to shower and scrub her abdomen three times with the solution that I would leave on the rim of the tub. After her family left, she went into the bathroom and saw the cup sitting there. She said she paused for a moment and tried to remember what I had told her. Then, looking at the solution in the cup, she picked it up and drank it."

"Then what did you do?" I inquired.

"I hurried and told my preceptor."

The preceptor called the pharmacist, and he indicated probably no harm was done.

"Now I have to fill out an incident report."

After filling out the incident report, Sue sighed, "Well! I learned at least two things today: make sure the patient understands my instructions and don't put anything in a cup that isn't for drinking."

This incident brought back a memory from many years ago: a sweet elderly couple stood looking at me, nodding and smiling as I explained to them about the wife's medication. The wife had come to the clinic complaining of spurts of shortness of breath and difficulty breathing. The resident physician had ordered aminophylline suppositories PRN whenever they were needed.

"She gets frightened when she can't breathe, and it scares me too," explained the husband in a heavy Hebrew accent, "She needs medicine."

"This is what these suppositories are for," I instructed.

With hand gestures and speaking slowly, I continued my instructions, "When she has difficulty breathing, you take off the wrapper and have her insert it into her rectum."

I cautioned that she was only to use the suppositories when she had an episode of shortness of breath or difficulty breathing. Both smiled and nodded, then smiled and nodded again seeming pleased with the medication I had handed them.

Two weeks later, I spotted the elderly couple as they were being ushered to a room for their appointment. Greeting them, I inquired if the medication had helped. With a half nod and a semi-smile the husband replied,

"Some. They were too big for her to swallow so she had to break them in half and chew them."

Oooh no! I thought and then proceeded to ask a silly question, "Didn't she complained they tasted bad?"

"Sometimes she did," the husband replied.

I don't remember who, but someone came to my rescue with a word that they would understand on how to administer the medication.

The Psalmist David reveals that, "[God] will teach you the way that you should go: and [He] will keep [His] eye on you and guide you along safe paths." Psalms 32:8

When I pay attention to God's instructions, my path is safe, but often I find myself like my patients: too preoccupied, not pausing long enough, too comfortable with the familiar, and sometimes even nodding and smiling, pretending I understand. The results? I might drink a solution intended for scrubbing and chew distasteful medicine that should have been administered in the opposite way.

Do Not Run

"Hi! I am Jennifer Saxton, a student nurse, and I will be taking care of you today. I am going to do a head-to-toe assessment. First, I am going to place a stethoscope on your chest and listen to your lungs and heart."

Jennifer listened carefully and reported that all sounds seemed to be normal. Then, she listened to his bowel sounds. For the neuro check, she instructed her patient to grip both of her hands, to touch his nose and to smile. Her patient, Mr. Webber, being blind, made Jennifer aware that she needed to explain her every move. He was a diabetic and had a large infected ulceration on his right leg. Jennifer commented step by step, telling him she was going to examine his leg ulcer, which she observed looked good and seemed to be healing well. Then, Jennifer told Mr. Webber she was going to get his breakfast tray.

When Jennifer reentered Mr. Webber's room, she did not introduce herself again, assuming he would recognize her voice. Placing the breakfast tray on his over-the-bed table, Jennifer took the plastic wrap off the silverware and the lid off his hot drink.

Not recognizing Jennifer's voice as she had assumed he would, Mr. Webber asked, "Who is your supervisor? There was a student in here looking at my wound, and it bothered her so I don't want her taking care of me."

"My first instinct was to run out of the room as fast as I could, find my nursing instructor and cry, 'My patient doesn't want me to take care of him!'" said Jennifer.

Instead, with all the composure she could muster up, Jennifer replied, "I am the student that looked at your wound and it didn't bother me; it looked good and seemed to be healing nicely. But if you would like, I will get another student to come in and take care of you."

"Oh! If it didn't bother you then it's okay," informed Mr. Webber.

Still feeling a little embarrassed over the situation, Jennifer continued with her care for Mr. Webber. It did not take long for Jennifer and Mr. Webber to get into some good conversations ranging from the mundane to the spiritual. They found they had many common interests. Jennifer stayed with Mr. Webber most of the morning, introducing herself every time she entered his room. At the end of the shift Mr. Webber mentioned that he enjoyed her and appreciated the good care she had provided and hoped she would be his nurse the next day.

"It felt good to know I did not run away from what seemed like a bad situation for me. It actually turned out to be a good experience, one I will always remember," said Jennifer.

How many times have we, like Jennifer, wanted to run from an unpleasant situation, particularly when it's a personal criticism? It takes a lot of composure to work through a tough situation. From where does that inner strength come?

Hopefully, we will be like the Psalmist David who in a tough situation (which seemed to be most of his life), would say with confidence, "The Lord guides those who depend on Him and gives them the help they need. The Lord helps the righteous and gives them support in times of trouble." Psalm 37: 23, 39.

When we draw strength from the right source as we face tough situations, perhaps we, too, can say as Jennifer did, "It actually turned out to be a good experience, one I will always remember."

Comfort Measures

The Way Home

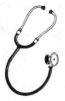

"Food, Fun, Forum!"

A catchy title? I thought so. Every so often, the nursing faculty would bring together the different levels of nursing students to clarify some expectations, e.g. expectations for their upcoming summer practicum, graduation requirements, or information regarding the NCLEX (the national licensing exam). There, the faculty would also encourage any questions or suggestions the students might have.

Well, the catchy title worked! The sessions were well attended and benefitted both faculty and students. They also enjoyed mingling over food and would have a good laugh together over a skit or video presentation from the upperclassmen. Needless to say, a lot of valuable feedback came from these sessions, which helped the faculty understand some of the students' problems as well as allowing the students to feel like they were making a positive contribution to the program.

As usual, at the end of one such session, the moderator encouraged suggestions or questions when a hand shot up from the back row.

"You give us excellent directions how to get to our clinicals, but you don't tell us how get back," lamented a fundamentals student.

Chuckling I thought to myself, *Well! Just go back the way you came.* I am now glad I did not make that comment, because on second thought, I realized the metropolitan area where the majority of the clinical sites were located were one-way streets. Traveling to the clinical area would take you one way, but returning was a different story. Exiting the clinical area required a quick maneuver to the far left-hand lane of a four-lane road. Then, one would have to cut through a residential street to another main thoroughfare, going one way. However, this thoroughfare dead-ended into another major road so a left-hand turn was required. Then, in a few blocks, one would have to ease right to go back to the road that one came on to finally be able to return to the university. Complicated? Yes! Even though it sounded silly at first, it was a legitimate comment.

We should pray as King David did, "Lord, help me know your way and give me strength to follow it and do what is right." (Psalm 5:8)

Keep in mind that God never thinks we are silly for asking for directions. For He promises that, "He will lead [us] along roads we have not known and guide [us] along paths that are new. He will turn darkness into light and make the rough spots smooth, and not forsake us." (Isaiah 42:16)

When asking God for directions, here is a sobering thought: "My thoughts are not your thoughts, neither are my ways your ways."

But the good news is that "as the heavens are higher than the earth, so are [His] thoughts higher than [our] thoughts and [His] ways higher than [our] ways." (Isaiah 55:8)

Probably the most comforting promise of all when we need directions is found in that most familiar Psalm—Psalm 23.

Psalms 23 tells us that He leads us beside quiet waters, walks with us through a valley of frightful shadows when facing death. His rod and staff protect us. His goodness and mercy will be with us every day of our lives.

God bids us to daily ask for instructions.

"So make God's kingdom and His righteousness first in your life, and all the other things will be given to you as you need them." (Matthew 6:33)

"Other things," as mentioned in the previous passage, include the promise in Isaiah 30:21, "If you start turning to the right or to the left you will hear a still, small voice telling you, 'Over here is the way to walk.'"

Now *that* is the best way home!

Plans

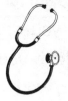

Craig had been planning a career in anesthesia for several years. He had even moved from the comforts of home to a large, strange city to work in intensive care units in the hospital where the school of anesthesia of his choice was located. He chose this particular location because this school of anesthesia offered a Bachelor of Science degree, a rarity back then. After working for several years, he applied to the school of anesthesia. His interview with the faculty was a very positive experience and he felt fairly confident he would be one of the four candidates that would be accepted.

This confidence did not last long, for in a few weeks he suffered the disappointment of not being admitted to the program. His blighted hope was somewhat lessened by the conviction that God was still leading in the direction of anesthesia and the fact that the faculty had told him he would be a priority candidate when he reapplied next year. He continued to work in an intensive care unit, eagerly anticipating the next spring when he would be admitted to the anesthesia program.

In May of the next year, the acceptance letters were sent out. Craig could not believe his eyes as he read that he had been placed on the alternate list. Being first alternate did not diminish his devastating disappointment. Being his mother, I felt his keen disappointment. As we talked on the phone, I was searching for something comforting to say.

"Maybe one of the candidates will have to drop out before next fall," I suggested trying to sound optimistic.

"Well! That is very unlikely since it is so difficult to be admitted to an anesthesia program these days," he groaned.

Before hanging up, I promised Craig that I would continue to pray for him and his career choice and that the Lord would give him peace of mind and wisdom for the future. Even though he was somewhat disillusioned, he said he had already committed his situation to the Lord and asked for guidance.

"Craig got into anesthesia school," were the first words that greeted me upon my return from vacation.

It seemed that my oldest son was just as excited as Craig was about the news. It turned out that one of the candidates had applied to two schools of anesthesia. This candidate notified the school of anesthesia where Craig had applied that he had been accepted in another school and wanted to withdraw his name. Now, Craig, being the first alternate could take his place.

When Craig called to discuss the quick change in events he humbly confessed, "Even though my faith that God was leading in my life never wavered, this experience has taught me a valuable lesson: 'The best laid plans of mice and men' can go afoul and the future at times can appear pretty dismal, but God is still in charge."

"Commit your way unto the Lord; trust also in Him; and he shall bring it to pass," Psalms 36:5.

"Delight thyself also in the Lord; and he shall give you the desires of your heart," Psalms 37:4

Isn't there a lesson here for all of us?

Prayer
a Must

Near Misses

The memory of the incident still haunts me. Christy Hayes, student nurse, had just received report on her patients when surgery called and said they were coming to pick up one of Christy's patients. Since this was the students' first day for this particular rotation, I assisted Christy with preparing the patient, Mrs. Eaves, for surgery. We dashed around checking to see if the permit was signed and the lab work was on the chart. Christy drew up the pre-op medication, checked for nail polish, make-up and that Mrs. Eaves had emptied her bladder. The orderly appeared at the door with the gurney, so Christy quickly administered the pre-op medication. Then, it was with frightened eyes that Mrs. Eaves looked at us and asked,

"Are you Christians?"

"Yes," we replied in unison.

"Then pray for me! Quick!"

Startled, Christy and I shamefully looked at each other. Quickly regaining our composure, Christy offered a prayer for the patient's safety in surgery and for a quick recovery. Thanking us for the prayer and looking somewhat relieved, Mrs. Eaves was rolled out of the room on the gurney and down the hall to surgery. After talking with the family for a few minutes and still feeling a little awkward over the incident, we hastily exited the room.

"I hope I don't ever do that again—be so busy doing the one-two-threes of my duties and overlook the patient's need for me to pray with them," groaned Christy.

I told Christy that I, too, felt sad that we had not sensed Mrs. Eaves' need for spiritual care.

It had been one of those shifts that one tends to think will never get under control: a fresh surgery patient's blood pressure dropping precipitously, another patient's temperature rising to 104.2° with blood cultures to be drawn and then STAT antibiotics, a patient receiving chemotherapy accidentally pulled out her IV line, and two new admissions. I only had time for a hasty check here and there on Mrs. Hawkins as she lay there alone in her room. She was quiet, except for an occasional moan, as she drifted in and out of a semi-stuporous state. It was the end of the shift, yet I was still feeling rushed and frustrated. I was tempted to clear Mrs. Hawkins's IV pump quickly, empty her Foley catheter, and be on my way, but the incident with Christy flashed through my mind. Also, a saying I had read for my devotion that morning popped into my head, *you can always pray for someone when you don't have the strength to help him in some other way.*

I knew I had to take the time to comfort her.

"Mrs. Hawkins, would you like for me to pray for you?" I whispered in the ear of this frail, dying elderly lady.

To my surprise, she opened her eyes and nodded her head.

"Dear Jesus, send comfort, peace and a good night's rest for this precious soul," my voice cracking, I continued, "May she rest in the promise that you will be with her always. Amen."

During the prayer Mrs. Hawkins started to sob uncontrollably. I held her hand and patted her shoulder trying to comfort her to no avail. The sobbing went on for quite some time. I began to wonder if I had done more harm than good. Finally, the sobbing quieted. Feeling distressed that I might have caused her more grief than anything, I left the room.

Later Mrs. Hawkins' family told me that after I prayed, Mrs. Hawkins told them she drifted off in a more peaceful sleep and rested better that night. Sadly a few days later, she slipped into a coma and died.

Sue Allen, a nursing instructor, and a student went to remove a nasal gastric feeding tube from Mrs. King, a patient who had just recently started to tolerate oral nourishment. Mrs. King had a malignancy and had endured many painful, unpleasant procedures.

After the student explained what she was going to do, Mrs. King looked up at Sue and pleaded, "Oh, pray it won't hurt."

Quietly, Sue took Mrs. King's hand, closed her eyes, and bowed her head briefly. After a moment she opened her eyes to see Mrs. King's eyes fixed on her.

"That was an awfully short prayer," complained Mrs. King. Gently squeezing Mrs. King's hand, Sue whispered, "God hears short prayers too!"

The nasal gastric tube was removed without difficulty.

Months later, Sue was making rounds when she entered the room of Mrs. King who had been readmitted to the hospital. The cancer had taken its toll, for there lay Mrs. King with a large swollen abdomen, her arms and legs just skin and bones. Sue hardly recognized her.

Surprised to see Sue, Mrs. King summoned a weak smile and then asked Sue if she would pray for her again.

"I would like to do just that," responded Sue.

Tearfully, Sue asked God to bring comfort and peace to Mrs. King. Opening her eyes this time Sue saw Mrs. King slowly and with great effort raise her emaciated hand to gently pat Sue on the cheek.

In recent years, faith, prayer and illness have been of interest to researchers. One conclusion is that prayer has obvious appeal: it is easy-to-use, inexpensive and has no apparent side effects. Even skeptics conclude that it won't hurt to try. Prayer can give hope and encouragement while reducing anxiety.

Holy Scriptures command us to pray without ceasing and to pray one for another. Then, it rewards us with the promise that the fervent prayer of a righteous man has tremendous power. (James 5:16)

"Can We Pray?"

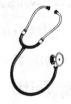

"Can we pray?"

"Oh my, yes!"

"In the confusion of the moment I almost forgot. I am so thankful you remembered," I sheepishly replied to Tina's request.

Tina was just leaving my office to go to the testing center to take her NCLEX (National Council Licensure Examination) to become a registered nurse when several faculty and classmates, who had already taken the exam, stopped by to wish her well. There were lots of hugs, gleeful chatter, and "you can do it" encouragements.

During the summer, I tutor and mentor students preparing for this very important examination and faithfully pray with each one just prior to them taking the exam. Now, here was Tina, who had been a special challenge, and I was about to forget the most important preparation of all: prayer.

Earlier in the summer, Tina had mentioned that she was trying to get her spiritual life back on track, because she felt it would help her depression. Tina had admitted to having no motivation to prepare for NCLEX. She said she tried but couldn't even force herself to study. The only motivation she had was to come to my office several times a week for study sessions. The first part of these study sessions consisted of her deploring the fact that she had no motivation, yet knew she had to prepare for the exam to be successful. The next part of the study session was me nagging, "Tina, just force yourself to practice 50 questions in the morning and 50 questions in the afternoon and pretty soon you will become more motivated to practice more."

Then we would end a session practicing NCLEX-type questions together, which indicated her need for more earnest preparation.

The faculty in the School of Nursing where I teach has taken seriously the injunctions to "always have a prayerful attitude" (1Thessalonians 5:17), to "pray for each other" and are encouraged that "the fervent prayer of a righteous man has tremendous power." (James 5:16)

To communicate this philosophy on a practical level, the School of Nursing has made a practice of putting on a bulletin board, where faculty offices are located, the names of students with the scheduled dates and times of their NCLEX exam. On the date of a student's exam there is a special spot on the bulletin board for their name to be placed with the time of the exam. This very visible spot enables the faculty to view who is taking the exam and the time so they can say a special prayer at that time. After receiving notice of their success there is a "congratulations" spot for their name, which is cause for great rejoicing. The students know that we do this and say they are very comforted by this practice. They even say they feel this is one reason they have been successful on NCLEX!

Sadly, Tina had to remind me of this commitment to pray, especially for her at this most stressful time. After claiming God's promise to give wisdom to those who ask and asking for God to send a calming spirit on Tina, she left the office a little nervous but smiling and hopeful of conquering the challenge.

Tina was successful on her NCLEX— "fervent" prayer does have tremendous power.

O Death, Where is Thy Sting

"Though I walk through the Valley of the Shadow of Death..."

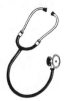

The patient was gasping for breath and clutching his chest, eyes rolling toward the back of his head. Members of his family who were standing by his bedside were ringing their hands, sobbing loudly, and I, the student nurse, who was sent to observe someone dying, was standing close by wondering why someone or something couldn't be done to help this pitiful soul. When the gasping subsided, the patient went limp, then the family wailed all the louder. I slipped out of the room having no idea of what to do since I had only been hustled in to witness death taking place.

This was in the days before CPR (Cardio Pulmonary Resuscitation) and the concept of letting one die with dignity. When I asked what caused the man's death, I think they said something about his heart, but I don't really remember for sure. But I do remember that, unfortunately, this experience formed my image of how one goes about the process of dying. It left me confused about the notion that when one dies they just "fall asleep in Jesus."

Even at forty, she was too young to be dying of colon cancer. I'm not sure how long the battle against this monster of a disease had been, but my first encounter with Marlene was a few days after she had been admitted to the hospital for the last agonizing days of her life. I don't know why I used the word "agonizing" to describe her last days—I guess I used that word because it was agonizing for the family and for me. Actually, Marlene was quite at peace with the experience. It was the peaceful expression on her face that always caught me off guard as she lay quietly in bed with her hands folded over her chest. As I performed her daily assessment, I would ask if there was anything I could do for her. Sometimes she would ask to be turned or request a sip of water, or would just give a weak smile and say she was "all right for now."

Since I worked the evening shift, her husband would fill me in on what kind of day she'd had and then before leaving the room, I would pat her arm and tell her I would check on her frequently.

One evening, as I was preparing to leave her room, she opened her eyes and looked up at me and said,

"I like your wig."

I smiled and whispered, "It's not a wig it's my real hair."

She responded, "That's okay, I have one just like it at home."

I marveled to myself that this dying woman had the strength to comment on my hair. Wow!

The very next evening after doing her assessment, it seemed that she would not last through the night. She was so weak she could barely open her eyes to acknowledge my presence. I checked on her and her husband more frequently that evening feeling certain that it would be the last time I'd see them.

To my surprise, when I arrived the next evening, I saw that Marlene was still in her room. I quietly entered finding her respirations were shallow and weak and she seemed to be hanging on "by a thread," as the expression goes. Taking her wrist to feel for a pulse, she opened her eyes, looked up at me and weakly but quite audibly said,

"I fooled you. I'm still here."

I couldn't help but smile and think "wow" again—this woman still had a sense of humor. I was off the next day and the nurse that took care of her during the night said that she just quietly "slipped away" in the early morning. It amazed me how Marlene had accepted her immortality in such a quiet, unassuming way, so unlike the experience I had witnessed as a student.

Even though I went off to graduate school and focused on oncology nursing, I never ceased to be surprised by how my patients dealt with death and dying, again, so unlike the experience I had as a student. Once, I walked in a room to check on a dying patient and found the patient telling her husband where to look in the closet for the outfit she wanted to be buried in.

I went away wondering how one could make such plans as life is ebbing away. One wife, just a few weeks before her death, made a prioritized list of women for her husband to consider marrying after she died. She was suffering with pancreatic cancer and knew her death would not be easy. I was puzzled by how she could be worrying about her husband's welfare at a time like this.

Another time, I entered a patient's room to find eight people crammed around the bedside of this dying relative. Mostly they were talking among themselves but occasionally would include the patient by asking if she remembered so-and-so or to ask her a question. Even though she was very weak, the patient would try to respond. As I did my assessment, I sensed all these people were making her anxious. I asked her if she wanted them to leave the room for a while. She shook her head, "no." A few minutes later I had to hang some IV fluids, and I continued to sense she was anxious so I asked her again if she would like for her family to leave the room, this time she nodded "yes." The family all got up, left the room but stood around in the hall by her door. I followed them out.

About three or four minutes later I noticed one of the relatives with a bewildered look on her face peeking in the room. I went back into the room and checked on the patient. She had died. The relative that had been peeking in the room looked at me in astonishment and said, "She wanted us out so she could die in peace, didn't she?"

And that was the way it seemed. With everyone out of the room, she could relax and let go peacefully.

My concept of how one goes about the process of dying has changed rapidly over time. I've observed that all these patients had come to grips with the inevitable.

Death and dying, like birthing, are part of the cycle of life.

What gave them acceptance was their belief in God and His promise that, "The Lord is my shepherd I will lack nothing. He lets me lie down in green pastures. He leads me beside quiet water. He restores the strength of my soul. He guides me along paths of righteousness. Even when I have to walk through a valley of frightful shadows facing death, I will fear no evil, because you are with me. Your rod and staff protect me. Your goodness and mercy will be with me every day of my life, and I will live with you in your house forever." (Psalm 23)

Evidence of their faith was seen in the spiritual artifacts around their room as well as patients, family members and me sharing our favorite texts with each other, which most often in these circumstances was the twenty-third Psalm.

A Familiar Affair

The Duffs

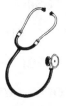

There were eight of them. First, it was Donny, who was always smiling and courteous—a delight to have in the nursing program. Then, Donna, a nursing classmate, captured his fancy and after graduation they married, which made for two nurse Duffs.

Two years later, Pat came along, who was also always smiling and courteous. He took a liking to nursing classmate, Sandy, and they were married after graduation, making four nurse Duffs. While Pat was in his senior year, mother Duff, Barbara, decided to take nursing. She took an accelerated class and graduated just one year behind Pat, making five nurse Duffs.

Within a few years, Andy, the youngest son, who couldn't resist the call to nursing, met Sibby, a nursing classmate, and after graduation, they married, making seven nurse Duffs. Before Andy completed his nursing education, father Don lost his job and not knowing what else to do at the time he enrolled in the nursing program. He graduated about a year after his son, Andy, making eight nurse Duffs all from the same nursing program—a record, I am sure.

Even though I did not mention that mother, Andy, and father were smiling and courteous, they were, and were much more. The Duffs are portraits of the very essence of Christian service and in the following stories you will see the unique ways God has used them and helped them in their careers.

Here are their stories...

Guardian Angel

Out of sorts for being pulled from the Cardiac Care Unit to the medical/surgical floor, Don started his rounds to assess his assigned patients in a grumpy mood. The first room he entered was Mr. MacGregor's. Don found him looking over a stack of "Texas Ranger" baseball cards, all personally signed. Instantly, Don's mood changed.

Mac, as he was affectionately called, was an unofficial mascot of the Texas Rangers, and Don was a huge fan of this baseball team. Mac had been visiting a patient in the hospital when he had an episode of syncope. He was taken to the

Emergency Department. Tests revealed he had suffered a minor myocardial infarction (MI) and was subsequently admitted to the medical/surgical floor for treatment and monitoring.

After assessing Mac, Don continued his rounds and went about providing the necessary nursing care to his patients. Whenever Don had a break in his duties that evening, he would stop in Mac's room and chat about the Texas Rangers. The next evening, during a break in his Cardiac Care Unit routine, Don took time to go back to visit with Mac, thus beginning a special friendship.

After Mac's discharge from the hospital, he kept in touch with Don. Mac felt Don's interest in him and friendship contributed to his speedy recovery. Often, they went to Texas Ranger games together since Mac always had an extra ticket to share. The two simply enjoyed each other and had a great time visiting together.

Donna, Don's wife, was an emergency room nurse and had taken a few days off to do some things around the apartment with the help of her cousin. Needing some curtain rods, they hurried off to a local hardware store. After looking over every rod available, they finally made a selection. Just after paying for their purchase, they heard someone yell,

"We need help over here!"

Donna looked around and saw a man lying on the floor. She rushed over and found a man that was purple and unconscious.

"Call 911," she commanded.

Buttons flew everywhere as Donna ripped off the man's shirt to start CPR.

Two breaths, fifteen chest compressions; two breath, fifteen chest compressions.

"I hope those paramedics get here soon," Donna silently prayed.

Two breaths, fifteen chest compressions; two breaths, fifteen chest compressions, which was protocol at the time.

Finally, the paramedics arrived, started IV fluids, continued the CPR and rushed the man off to the hospital. Feeling that the man was in good hands now, Donna and her cousin headed home.

Upon arriving home, Don checked out the curtain rods and then asked,

"Did you see Mac? He works at the hardware store."

"No," Donna answered.

Then she told Don about having to provide CPR for a man in the hardware store.

"You don't suppose that was Mac, do you?" inquired Don.

"I don't think so, but it would have been difficult to tell since the man's face was all purple," replied Donna.

"I am going to call the emergency room and just check to see if it was Mac," responded Don.

Yes, he was informed, it was Mr. MacGregor that had suffered an MI in the hardware store,.

"He is being transferred to the Cardiac Care Unit. It's a good thing someone knew CPR in the store," said the nurse on the other end of the line, one of Donna's colleagues.

"The physicians say it saved his life. There doesn't appear to be any brain damage and that no doubt is related to his early resuscitation."

Mac had heart bypass surgery and his recovery was surprisingly uneventful. Now, he felt he had a special bond with Donna.

"She is my guardian angel," he delighted in saying whenever they were together, "Donna is my number one angel and Don is my number two angel."

However, there was one item he regretted, Donna had ripped all the buttons off his shirt and his wife had to sew them back on.

"See here, I still have that shirt," Mac would brag pointing to the shirt, "It's a reminder that I know MY guardian angel."

I like to think that when the Psalmist proclaimed, "[God] will send His angels to take charge and protect you," (Psalms 91:11) that He uses nurses to help accomplish this task.

Stories of angels impersonating medical professionals abound, but when nurses are referred to as "angels of mercy" it is the real thing, no impersonation. For everywhere everyday nurses take charge and protect their patients from harm and, yes, they even save lives.

Doing What Is Right

Pat was looking forward to his 7p–7a shift in the Cardiac Surgical Care Unit. It was Sunday, and most of the patients would be about two days post-op, which usually meant a shift he could just cruise along and enjoy for a change. Upon arriving, he discovered that three nurses were scheduled for a low census, but there were four patients. *Ugh*, and it was his turn to float. Even worse: he had to float to the Medical Intensive Care Unit where every patient was on a ventilator, had tubes coming out of every orifice and most were near death, it seemed. With a less than cheerful attitude, Pat shuffled over to MICU and received his assignment. Matters got worse when he was informed that the daughter of Mr. Carter, one of his assigned patients, was allowed to stay at her father's bedside for the night. Silently he fretted, *What happened to the usual rule of the scheduled 'ten-minute family time'?*

Right off the bat, things were hectic. Both of his patients were on ventilators with respiratory problems; both had naso-gastric tubes; both had urinary catheters; both had numerous IV medications that kept him "hopping."

Pat was frequently in and out of Mr. Carter's cubicle on one chore or the other— assessing, suctioning, irrigating, turning, and hanging IV medicines. He had little time to speak to the daughter, but even under these less than desirable circumstances, Pat always maintained his professional, competent and caring persona.

Feeling the effects of a strenuous shift, Pat was eagerly preparing to go home when the daughter of Mr. Carter came out of the cubicle and thanked him for the quality care he had provided for her dad. Even though Pat appreciated the gratitude, he was just thankful the shift was over, so he did not give much thought concerning her comment.

Later down the line, Pat applied to anesthesia school. About three months after working that "float" shift, he received notice that he was to come in for his interview before the School of Anesthesia board. As would be expected, Pat was nervous. The room where the interview was to take place was formal and intimidating. Solemn appearances of the board members as they sat around a large mahogany table did nothing to calm his nerves. The chairman of the board beckoned Pat to take the one lone seat in front of the table. As Pat sat down, he glanced around the table of board members. To his surprise, there sat the daughter who had stayed with Mr. Carter the night he had floated to MICU. After both Pat and Mr. Carter's daughter nodded in recognition, the interview began. During the intensive questioning, Mr. Carter's daughter made several positive comments on the excellent care Pat had provided her dad.

Trembling hands did not stop Pat from opening the much-anticipated envelope with the return address marked "School of Anesthesia."

"I'm accepted, I'm accepted!" Pat shouted to any- one within an earshot.

In a few minutes Pat's elation tempered as he acknowledged that the comments Mr. Carter's daughter made probably played a big part in his acceptance into the school of anesthesia.

Soberly, he remarked, "You just never know what influence your actions will have."

The first text that came to my mind as Pat related his story to me was, "Let your light so shine before men, that they may see your good works..." Matthew 5:16.

Then, I came across a statement the apostle Paul made in 2 Corinthians 8:21 that we all should be mindful that "we intend to do what is right not only in the Lord's sight, but also in the sight of others."

God's Answer

Mother Duff, Barbara, told me after graduating that she could not shake the questions,

"Now that I am a nurse, God, why am I one? What am I supposed to do?"

Not having any clear direction, she took a job in a Pediatric Hospital. Since one of her five children was medically handicapped, she reasoned that she would be able to understand the parents of medically challenged children.

When Andy heard his mother was going to work with pediatric patients, he presented her with the cleverest clip-on girl and boy dolls for her uniform. The clip-on dolls had movable arms, hands and were dressed in the cutest fashion. The girl was dressed in a plaid jumper and white shirt and the boy wore jeans, overalls and a plaid shirt. Barbara treasured these dolls and clipped them on her uniform every evening before leaving for her 11:00 p.m. to 7:00 a.m. shift.

One evening, as Barbara was beginning her shift, she was assigned to admit a child from the children's ER. When the child arrived, accompanied by her mother and grandmother, Barbara was taken aback at how beautiful this 3-year-old was—but, oh, how pale as well! The lab report revealed her hemoglobin was 1 gram and blood had been ordered to run though the night.

Sitting on her mother's lap, the child did not even wince when the IV was inserted and the blood transfusions started. As Barbara assessed the child frequently, she noted the child barely made any movement except for changing laps from the mother to the grandmother who themselves appeared to be in a state of shock. Barbara's heart went out to this distraught little family.

Toward morning, Barbara observed the transfusions must have done some good; now instead of white, there was a tinge of pink on the child's face. As she leaned over to listen to her little patient's heart and lungs, the little girl slowly reached out and touched the girl doll clipped on Barbara's uniform. Unclipping the doll from her uniform, Barbara handed it to this precious child. Clutching the doll in her tiny hand, the little patient snuggled closer to her mother and closed her eyes.

It was 4:45 a.m., Barbara said, when she looked up from her charting and there stood the mother, her lips quivering, inquiring if there was a place she could go and cry. Putting her arm gently around the mother, Barbara quietly ushered her to the nurses' lounge. For reasons she is not sure of, Barbara noted it was 5:55 a.m. when the mother, eyes swollen and red, came out of the nurses' lounge and thanked Barbara for her kindness and then told this story:

She and her daughter, Sarah, had come to visit the grandmother. The grandmother kept saying, "Sarah doesn't look good. You need to take her to see a doctor."

Finally, they called to make an appointment.

"It will have to be the last appointment of the day before the pediatrician could see her," they were told.

So, late that afternoon they had gone to the pediatrician's office. Confusion and shock set in as they heard words like, "Leukemia, blood transfusions, helicopter, St. Judes."

Comforting the mother the best she could, Barbara stayed over from her shift and assisted in transporting the child, who was still clutching that little doll, to the helicopter pad for the ride to St. Judes, the nationally known treatment center for childhood cancer. With a promise to keep her and her daughter in her prayers, Barbara bade them farewell and wearily started her trek home. As Barbara looked through the windshield at the bright cloudless morning, she glanced upward and murmured,

"God, was last night the reason you wanted me to be a nurse?"

Later after her sons Donny and Pat urged Barbara to broaden her nursing horizons, she took a job in a cardiac care unit. A young woman visiting her father, who had had a myocardial infarction, approached Barbara and inquired,

"Do you remember me?"

It was the mother of Sarah. Four years had passed and Sarah was in remission and doing great, said the mother. Then she added, "She still cherishes that little doll, and I will never forget your kindness in such a distressing experience."

"Everyone who asks will receive, and he who seeks will find, and for those who knock, the door will open." Luke 11:10.

While the World Partied

It was Christmas Eve and the emergency room was raging. Barbara had been called by an agency service to come and help out. After arriving, it was decided that the greatest need was to admit patients from the ER to the medical surgical floor.

At 11:45 p.m., a mom and dad arrived to the floor holding a frightened, dehydrated, septic young child with Down's Syndrome. Needle pricks dotted both hands and arms, markings of unsuccessful intravenous attempts. The physician on call had been notified of the situation. He said not to "stick" the child anymore and that he would come in the next day to insert the intravenous line.

The mom and dad were frantic to the point of despair. Here it was, Christmas Eve, they had other children at home, and they didn't know what to do. Should they have the dad go home and "do Christmas" with the other children at home, leaving mom and ill child at the hospital? Or, wait until later the next day when maybe mom could be there, too? Barbara knew all too well the difficulties a medically handicapped child presented.

When asking God why she was a nurse, Barbara always felt having a medically handicapped child herself would give her a special edge in situations like this. And actually, it had only been a few hours since Barbara was feeling sorry for herself. Her grown children were away for the holidays, and she and her nurse husband Don were scheduled to work. Barbara was called off, leaving her all alone on Christmas Eve, so she jumped at the chance to work when the agency called and asked her to go to this small, county hospital. Her spirit was quickly lifted as she listened to beautiful, soothing Christmas music on the ride to the hospital. Now facing this child whose temperature was 105 degrees, was dehydrated and septic and with no IV access for fluids, her spirit sank as fast as it had risen.

"He can't last through the night without intravenous fluids," she reasoned.

Assessing the child, Barbara saw a vein in his foot that just maybe would hold an intravenous needle. She decided to call the physician back and tell him that she did see a vein in the child's foot that might be accessed. While waiting for the physician to come to the phone, Barbara said she could hear a lot of gaiety: Christmas music playing, lively conversation, children squealing with delight, and the clinking of glasses and clanging of dishes—it seemed a good time was being had by all. When the physician finally came to the phone, Barbara informed him of the vein in the child's foot. After a long hesitation, the physician finally said okay, but only one stick.

Barbara immediately marched to the closest bathroom, fell to her knees and pleaded, "God, You know the desperate situation this little boy is facing; he needs fluids and antibiotics now. I can't do this, but you can! Amen."

Quietly gathering the IV fluid, tubing and 22 gauge angiocath, Barbara approached the frightened child. Explaining to the mom and dad the importance of not letting the boy move his foot, Barbara inserted the needle and immediately got a "flashback" of blood, then taped the site securely and started the fluids and antibiotic.

With the IV infusing without difficulty and the first dose of the IV antibiotic completed, Barbara busied herself admitting several more patients who had just been transferred from the ER.

When the chaos had quieted, Barbara went to check on the little Down's Syndrome patient. Stepping into the room, she noticed the mother had finally fallen sound asleep. Barbara took an extra blanket that was in the room and gently covered up the weary mother. As she paused at the door of the room and glanced back at the scene of this mother all alone in the room with a very ill, handicapped child on Christmas Eve, she thought about the contrast between the merriment she had heard in the home of the physician she had talked to earlier and the solemnity of the night Jesus was born: Mary, weary and alone, in a cattle stall with her first born Son using an animal's feeding trough for His cradle while the rest of the world partied.

God I Need You Again!

Intensive Care Unit.

Young man, quadriplegic, tracheostomy, septic, arms and legs so edematous no site for an intravenous could be found, waiting for a physician to insert a subclavian line.

In walks Barbara, fear staring at her—fear of a collapsed lung, fear of chest tubes, fear of dying. A previous experience had set the stage for fear to reap its havoc.

It was like déjà vu. On this young quad's last admission to ICU he needed intravenous fluids and no peripheral site for an IV could be located, so a subclavian line had been ordered resulting in a nicked lung, pneumothorax, chest tubes and one scared patient.

Compassionate Barbara thought, "There has to be some way a peripheral IV line can be started to avoid the trauma of a subclavian access." She found a quiet spot and prayed, *Lord, I need Your help. I cannot do this without You.*

Then, she reminded the Lord of the incident with the young Down's patient that also had no accessible IV site and He helped her to access a vein in his foot. Barbara recalled one of her nurse sons telling her, "In difficult situations, you can usually find good veins in the upper arms."

Collecting fluids, tubing and a 22-gauge angiocath Barbara prepared to start an IV in a very edematous arm where she could not see or feel a vein. Without using a tourniquet, Barbara inserted the 22-gauge angiocath in the young man's upper arm where she thought a vein should be and got an immediate "flashback." We ended with one relieved patient, one relieved nurse, and a "Thank You, Lord."

"With God, nothing is impossible." Luke 1:37

Desires of
the Heart

My Story

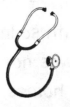

Humm, I don't think one can live on this, was the sinister thought flashing through my mind as I pondered over my first paycheck. Actually, I had been excited about my new nursing job after 21 years as a stay at home mom. Newly divorced with three-college age children living with me made going back to work more of a necessity than a novel idea.

I quickly rationed out the dollars for each expense: tithe, mortgage, utilities, food—just to cover the basics. Four hundred sixty-six dollars a month was not going to cut it, even with the children's father's commitment to paying their tuition.

Nevertheless, I had to accept the fact that these were the wages of a nurse in the seventies.

The excitement of working as a nurse was now mixed with sadness of my previous life lost. Money was not a particular issue then. Spacious homes, household help, country club memberships and children in private schools were the standard in our neighborhood and so it was with us.

Lounging by the pool of the country club while the children swam or played golf or tennis were almost daily occurrences during the summer. Sounds like the "good life," right? Wrong! Often, thoughts would plague me about doing something more constructive. I wasn't praying for something more constructive to do, but God, in His wisdom, gave it to me anyway.

Now, I was trying to keep life as normal as possible as I settled into my new, more constructive life, even though it wasn't close to the normal of the recent past. The children were busy with work and college but were missing the stay-at-home mom that cooked, cleaned, did the laundry and was always there to listen to the good and bad of the day. I would hurry home from work and try to have a good supper, but soon the chore of working and trying to keep life as it had been became a bit of a challenge.

That first pay check, especially, turned into a real reality check. From what seemed like the good life, I now felt I had been thrown to the sharks. I loved by job but getting up at five a.m. was torture for me. (I am not a morning person.) Now this: a salary that by no means could contend with the expense of everyday living.

What to do?

I turned all my concerns over to the Lord with total dependence on His promises to never, never abandon us. My faith was strong, but for some reason it did not stop me from crying and praying all the way to work each day. Eventually a certain amount of peace took over, and I quit fretting over every paycheck. Amazingly, bills got paid, tithe turned in and food remained on the table. Budget on paper said it wouldn't work, but it did.

Just before the fall session of college started (we moved in the summer), Steve my middle son announced, "Donny can't come to college unless he lives with us. His parents can't help with his tuition anymore. He will have to work his way through college."

Donny had been Steve's roommate in the private high school they attended.

Picture this: we are living in a postage stamp size house, budget beyond "tight," and I worked all day. My first inclination was, "No! No! No!" But with a little persuasion, I reconsidered. Fortunately My oldest son,

Rick, wanted to go back to the university he had been attending, so his bed was available.

After Donny, there was Peggy, then Carol, then Brian and finally, Rose.

"They can't come to college unless they live with us" was a refrain that I came to except as part of our "new" life.

"Mom that is a Charlie Brown Christmas tree," Bonnie Jeanne, the daughter of the family, lamented.

And it was. It was free, and that was all I could afford. However, it was kind of fun as we reminisced over the ornaments collected during their childhood. Don't ask me how, but somehow we scraped to gather enough money to join the college's ski club on their ski trip to Colorado right after opening gifts that first Christmas morning. This turned out to be a tradition for several Christmases that followed.

Eventually, the dawn broke into full sunlight and I realized my spiritual gift was serving others—my family, the staff and patients at work and later students. And *voila*! I could still do fun activities with the children. Now, this was the good life.

About two years into what I now refer to as "my new normal," Bonnie Jeanne came home from her summer college class with the following announcement: "They are hiring new faculty for the nursing department. You need to go and apply."

I did just that. I had commented several times that I would like to teach. That had been my goal when I graduated with my baccalaureate degree. Instead, I got married and started a family. Thus, the 21 years of being a stay-at-home mom.

Now, I had two years of very practical experience as a nurse that I figured should serve me well in teaching. I had committed my life to letting God guide me and my children to do His will. After applying for the teaching position, I left it in God's hands.

God is so good! I got the job! My first teaching assignment was patient care management. The wonder of wonders is that that was exactly what I had been doing, so my knowledge was very current on that aspect of nursing.

My first students and I had a great time, particularly during the clinical rotation. It turned out to be fun for the students and me. Since it was their last semester before graduating, the students were managing a group of patients and were feeling like a "real" nurse for the first time. They were performing all kinds of procedures that they hadn't had the opportunity to do before. The clinical rotations were exceptional because the staff nurses treated me as one of their own and would let me know of any extra procedures that the students could participate in. I knew in my heart of hearts that this was what the Lord wanted me to do.

Surprisingly, at the end of six years in our new life all three children had graduated from college and I had received my Master's degree in Nursing. A few years back, this would have seemed humanly impossible, but not so when God is on your side.

One morning, as I was hurrying to my office, I bumped into a former student that was now one of the nursing instructors. He greeted me with a question:

"Do you want to sell your house?"

"Yes, if you want to buy it," I responded.

David, the new faculty instructor had never seen my house and had no idea where I lived.

"Do you want to see my house?" I joked.

"Yes," he replied.

I took the house key off my key chain and gave him directions. The next thing I knew he was back and said, "I will take it."

This was the beginning of my house-building spree. I never ever set out to build houses. The next house I built was in a beautiful location, on top of a mountain near the college.

A few years later, déja vu: another "would you sell your house?" situation occurred.

Then came the next house, which was up the street from the last house, on the same mountain. Sold it in a few years. Next, I built closer to the university. After selling this fourth house, I built my retirement house on a mountain ridge with a spectacular view.

God works in mysterious ways. Not only did I beat the odds of living off of a salary that, on paper, indicated that it wouldn't work, but God threw in a bonus and gave me the desires of my heart:

I was born and raised in flat Florida but vacationed in the mountains of North Carolina. I dreamt that someday, I would actually live on top of a mountain. When I was a stay at home mom, the notion of teaching nursing one day seemed like a dream lost. As I prayed for my children, I wondered what God had in store for them. Now they are successful Christians with families of their own.

God is faithful with his promises: if you "trust in the Lord and do good... He shall give you the desires of your heart." (Psalm 27: 3,4)

P.S.

As I reread my story I thought, *Readers are going to think this is a "Pollyanna" story.* Not so! Every step of my journey has had its trials: more difficult situations then finances to deal with, and on top of it all, my prayers, many times, seemed to go unanswered. Of course, in retrospect, I can see that all my prayers were answered even if the answer was "no." With the "no" prayers, God had something far greater for me than I could ever have imagined. Now, in my retirement, I can see that God continues to give me a rewarding, productive life as a coordinator of an assisted learning program for the School of Nursing at Southern

Adventist University, where I taught for 20 years, as well as continuing to fulfill the promise to provide "the desires of my heart" in other areas.

Writing this book, which reflects some of the challenging, rewarding and humorous experiences of my teaching career, is another fulfillment for the "the desires of my heart.

Retirement

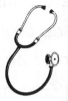

The last year before retirement, I prayed God would guide me to what I should do in my retirement.

During my teaching career, I worked one shift per week in a local hospital to keep up my nursing skills. My plans were to continue with one shift every week and thought that perhaps I would help in the local soup kitchen for the homeless as community service. Those were not God's plans.

Nursing students endure a rigorous education. Classroom theory has to be put into practice. An older Hispanic student was having difficulty with the theory aspect of her nursing studies in her Associate's level classes. I was teaching on the Baccalaureate level so did not have any contact with her. She had seen me around, and one day at church asked if she could talk with me. A simple, "Sure I would be happy to talk with you," led to what God had planned for my retirement.

Outside of work for the next two years, I would meet with her at home or during walks on the university track. The drill was for me to quiz her about the nursing content of the particular section she was in and showing her how this applied clinically.

When I announced my retirement, frequently the faculty asked, "Wouldn't other students benefit from this same kind of mentoring?"

"Yes, it would be very beneficial," was my consistent reply.

"Would you consider managing a mentoring program for the school of nursing when your retire," was the next question that emerged from every faculty meeting before my retirement.

I didn't consent until one night just after going to bed, a light bulb went off in my head, and the thought came that maybe this was what God wanted me to do in my retirement—another career was in the making.

Now, I coordinate a program for assisting students to achieve professionally (ASAP). I facilitate review sessions on classroom theory and help the students to pull it all together for clinical use and on tests. Reviewing test questions to help students develop good test taking skills also became a part of assisting them to achieve their goal for a career in nursing.

Helping in the community soup kitchen did not seem to fit my schedule. However, thoughts that I should do some kind of community outreach would plague me every now and then. One day, a former nursing graduate walked in my office and asked if I would tutor her to prepare for the national exam nursing (NCLEX) graduates have to take to become registered nurses. She had failed already, twice.

Since my daytime hours were filled with ASAP, I scheduled to meet with her in the evenings, and since I had been assisting students with test taking skills, I figured it would come in handy in helping this former graduate.

Before I even started with that first tutoring session, two additional nursing graduates that had failed the national exam wanted to join in the sessions. It was not an easy process. These gals needed a lot more than test-taking skills, they needed a good theory review. It literally took months to prepare them to retake the exam. After they were successful on the exam, went to work in local hospitals and found graduates from other nursing programs that were not successful on the exam, they told them about how I had helped them.

Before I could catch my breath from the previous tutoring sessions, I had a room full of girls and guys from various nursing schools in the area that had not been successful on the exam. Meeting in the evenings twice a week over many months was just as rewarding for me as it was for these aspiring nurses. It was interesting to see this very culturally diverse group bond and share life stories. However, they all had one thing in common: passing the NCLEX.

Six nurses from India that had to pass the national exam before they could practice nursing here in the US were included in the culturally diverse bunch. These gals and guys were such a blessing to me. My mother was living with me and was dying from congestive heart failure. The nurses from India wanted to visit my home and pray over my mother. They prayed in unison, and though it was difficult to understand what they were praying, it was sweet music to my ears. Now, they are nurses filling important roles in various hospitals in the community. One of the male nurses from India that attended review sessions even returned to the university to earn a Master's degree in nursing.

When I prayed for God to guide me in my retirement, it brought to mind Jabez's prayer for God to enlarge his territory and it reminded me that God's "hand would be with me, and that [He] would keep me from evil, that I may not cause pain." 1Chronicles 4:10

God certainly enlarged my territory, and my prayer is that I cause no pain along the way.

Acknowlegements

The saying "it takes a village to raise a child"... well it literally took a village to publish this book. Simone Marshall a talented journalism graduate from Southern Adventist University assisted with the editing and formatting. Inspired by the Twitter name of a former nursing student Rebecca Gates/ Lewis, Simone help create the title "Called to Care." Savaging me from many difficult computer situations is by dear Colleague Diane Proffitt, who saw to it that the manuscript was transported to its proper place. Friend and colleague Dana Krause lent her talents with providing the graphics and Jim Marlow tried his best to make me look good for the back cover photo. A shout out to David Gerstle, PhD, RN for the effort he put in to publish

2 editions of inspirational stories about nurses ("Inspiration PRN," "Jesus Prays With Us") that we co-authored...thus preserving many of the stories I have included in "Called To Care."

A special appreciation is given to those who so generously shared their experiences with me for this book: relatives, friends, colleagues and students. Many of the stories are from my own experience in addition to some ideas that have come from inspirational articles (tattered and torn from age and unknown sources) that I shared with the students over many years of teaching. A diligent effort has been made to give proper credit in the following acknowledgments:

Bible texts are quoted from the New King James (NKJ) and from the Clear Word (CW).

"Jesus Cares," Carole D. Hicks, *Polk County News*, August 17, 2005 p. 5.

Florence Nightingale Becomes a Nurse, some of the content was gleaned from an article by Paul Chrastina. source unknown.

Life is Backwards, Laura Billings, St. Paul Pioneer Press, May 2001.

Good Medicine: A patient rang his call light, A nursing assistant tells..., An ER nurse tells..., Mark was born with one ventricle..., Art Linkletter tours a nursing home... were all taken from the *Journal of Nursing Jocularity. The Humor Magazine for Nurses. V.7#3 Fall 1997, V. #2 Summer1996, V.6 #2 Summer 1996, V.7 #3 Fall 1997, V. 3 #4 Winter 1993.*

Thank a Nurse: The essence of these stories came from articles by:

Linda Chitwood *CATS, PETS, AND MRIs Don't Supply the Care: Nurses Do.* Source unknown

Dr. Thomas, author of the book *The Youngest Science. Viking press, February 1982*